INDIVIDUALISED MATHEMATICS

SES

**Developed by the School Ma
association with the Nationa**

CW00841641

MATRIX ALGEBRA AND ISOMETRIC TRANSFORMATIONS

CAMBRIDGE UNIVERSITY PRESS

**Cambridge
London New York New Rochelle
Melbourne Sydney**

The School Mathematics Project

When the SMP was founded in 1961, its main objective was to devise radically new secondary school mathematics courses to reflect, more adequately than did the traditional syllabuses, the up-to-date nature and usages of mathematics.

SMP Books 1–5 form a five-year course leading to the O-level examination in SMP Mathematics. *Revised Advanced Mathematics Books 1, 2 and 3* cover the syllabus for the A-level examination in SMP Mathematics. Five shorter texts cover the material of the various sections of the A-level examination SMP Further Mathematics. There are two books for SMP Additional Mathematics at O-level. All the SMP GCE examinations are available to schools through any of the GCE examining boards.

Books A–H cover broadly the same development of mathematics as the first few books of the O-level series. Most CSE boards offer appropriate examinations. In practice, this series is being used very widely across all streams of comprehensive schools and its first seven books, together with *Books X, Y and Z*, provide a course leading to the SMP O-level examination. *SMP Cards I and II* provide an alternative treatment in card form of the mathematics in *Books A–D*. The six units of *SMP 7–13*, designed for children in that age-range, provide a course for middle schools which is also widely used in primary schools and the first two years of secondary schools. Teacher's guides accompany all these series.

The SMP has produced many other texts, and teachers are encouraged to obtain each year from the Cambridge University Press, P.O. Box 110, Cambridge CB2 3RL, the full list of SMP publications currently available. In the same way, help and advice may always be sought by teachers from the Executive Director at the SMP Office, Westfield College, Kidderpore Avenue, London NW3 7ST. The annual Reports, details of forthcoming in-service training courses and other information may be obtained from the SMP Office.

The SMP is continually evaluating old work and preparing for new. The effectiveness of the SMP's work depends, as it has always done, on the comments and reactions received from teachers and pupils in a wide variety of schools using SMP materials. Readers of the texts can, therefore, send their comments to the SMP in the knowledge that they will be taken into consideration.

The authors of the original books on whose work this series is based are named in *The School Mathematics Project: The First Ten Years*, published by the Cambridge University Press.

SMP Individualised Mathematics has been produced by a team consisting of

Judy Bonsall	G. Merlane
G. S. Howlett	L. Savins
M. K. Leach	D. R. Skinner
J. L. Lloyd	J. V. Tyson

John Lloyd led the work on the series until his death in 1977, and the final editing has been carried out by Derek Skinner. Many others have helped with advice and criticism, particularly those students who worked through the material in draft form.

Contents

Preface

SMP Individualised Mathematics is based upon the content of *SMP Books 1–5* and *Books A–G, X, Y, Z*, covering the syllabus for the O-level SMP Mathematics. There are two main distinguishing features of the series. First, the material is presented in a programmed form and the books are thus suitable for use in individualised learning, where self-assessment and clear explanation play a major role. The carefully structured development of each topic makes the books suitable for use by students working alone with minimum tuition, in schools, technical colleges, colleges of further education and on courses organised by the National Extension College.

Secondly, instead of the spiral development of the SMP texts, *SMP Individualised Mathematics* presents the mathematics by topics. Each book, apart from the two devoted to revision, presents the work on a particular theme. Hence the books will prove useful to pupils who have missed work through absence from class, to students coming from abroad, and to pupils transferring to a different school. The style and arrangement of these books should make them very suitable for use by pupils in the sixth form who are working to improve their earlier performance at CSE or O-level. The books will also be useful for revision and consolidation.

Although written with the SMP O-level course in mind, *SMP Individualised Mathematics*, like other SMP texts, can be used to prepare for other O-level examinations based on similar syllabuses.

The titles in this series are as follows.
Computation and Graphs
Probability and Statistics
Algebra 1: Language and Structure
Algebra 2: Equations, Formulas and Graphs
Further Algebra and Computation
Matrix Algebra and Isometric Transformations
Further Matrices and Transformations
Geometry 1: Symmetry and Trigonometry
Geometry 2: Shapes and Similarity
Geometry 3: Three Dimensions
Revision 1
Revision 2

How to use this book

Each chapter begins with a list of what you should be able to do after studying the chapter. This is followed by a pre-test, which gives you some idea of
what you should know before you start that particular chapter. If you have
difficulty with the pre-test you should revise the work required for it – from
either the appropriate chapter of this or a companion book, or an elementary
text-book – before continuing with the chapter.

The teaching part of the chapter is divided into several sections, and includes
a number of exercises. Other questions are asked in the text, and *you should
write down the answers to all these questions and exercises in a notebook* as
you go along. The start of each set of questions is marked by a white triangle
on the left-hand side of the page. When you come to a triangle with a number
in it (on the right-hand side of the page), you should check your work up to
that point by turning to the answers at the end of the chapter and finding the
triangle with the same number (now on the left-hand side of the page).

The teaching part of the chapter is followed by a summary of the important
results of the chapter (you may well find it helpful to copy these into a
separate notebook that is kept especially for revision), and a post-test to test
your understanding of the chapter as a whole. The answers to this post-test
are also at the end of the chapter.

Finally (apart from the answers) there is an assignment. This is another
exercise covering the whole chapter, but this time there are no answers in
this book. If at all possible you should have *this* exercise marked by a teacher
or tutor.

Information matrices

Objectives

This is what you should be able to do after studying this chapter.
(1)   Define a matrix.
(2)   Identify the rows, columns, and order of a matrix.
(3)   Recognise a square matrix and identify its leading diagonal.
(4)   Write down the one-stage route matrix for a network, and draw the network from a one-stage route matrix.
(5)   Write down the two-stage route matrix for a network.
(6)   Construct the three main types of incidence matrix for a given network, and draw the networks corresponding to given incidence matrices.

Pre-test

Not much mathematics is required to start this chapter! Provided you can count, add, subtract and multiply numbers, and extract information from a table of numbers, you are ready to start.

> **1**   Figure 1 below is a diagrammatic representation of part of British Rail's Inter-City network.

Which of the following questions can be answered *from the diagram?*

(a)   Which is nearer to London, Swansea or Swindon?

(b)   Which is nearer to London, Cardiff or Exeter?

(c)   If you are travelling from Paddington to Penzance, must you pass through Plymouth?

(d)   Is Exeter due south of Swindon?

(e)   In how many different directions can you leave Reading on an Inter-City train?

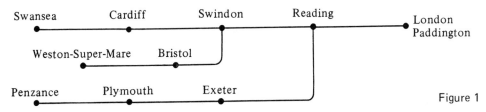

Figure 1

1

2   On Monday Tom spends 2 hours studying, $1\frac{1}{2}$ hours watching TV and $2\frac{1}{2}$ hours travelling. On Tuesday he spends $1\frac{1}{4}$ hours studying, $\frac{1}{2}$ hour watching TV and $1\frac{3}{4}$ hours travelling. The figures for Wednesday are $\frac{3}{4}$ hour studying, no TV, and $2\frac{1}{4}$ hours travelling; and for Thusday 1 hour studying, 1 hour TV, and 2 hours travelling.

      Work out the total time that he spent on each of these activities during the four days

3   I buy four books at £3.95 each, three shirts at £7.75 each and eight ties at £1.20 each. Find the total cost.

1.1 Information tables

Here are two more questions, slightly more complicated.

1   The results of four London football clubs after the first part of a season were

	Won	Drawn	Lost	Points
West Ham	9	5	6	
Spurs	6	5	8	
Arsenal	6	4	9	
Chelsea	3	8	8	

Complete the points column, using the scoring system of 2 points for a win, 1 for a draw and 0 for a loss.

2   A housewife's regular shopping order is 2 loaves of bread, 250 g of butter, 100 g of tea and 3 pints of milk. In 1975 a loaf of bread cost 8p, 1 kg of butter cost 64p, 1 kg of tea cost 50p and milk was 6p a pint. In 1980 the corresponding prices were 29p, 144p, 160p and 17p. Work out the total cost to the housewife (a) in 1975, (b) in 1980.

   The arithmetic involved in these examples is not too hard. Difficulty is more likely to arise in understanding the data (i.e. the information given in the question), and in sorting out the data and the steps in the calculation. In this chapter we shall consider a way of arranging some kinds of numerical data that will, with practice, help in this understanding and sorting out.

   Of the questions that we have looked at so far, the information is clearest in the one concerning football matches. However, we can display the data of the other questions in a similar manner. For example, the allocation of Tom's time in question 1 of the pre-test could be set out as

	Hours spent		
	studying	watching TV	travelling
Monday	2	$1\frac{1}{2}$	$2\frac{1}{2}$
Tuesday	$1\frac{1}{4}$	$\frac{1}{2}$	$1\frac{3}{4}$
Wednesday	$\frac{3}{4}$	0	$2\frac{1}{4}$
Thursday	1	1	2

In such tables the numbers are set out in *rows* and *columns*. A *row* runs across the page. For example, the second row is

$$1\tfrac{1}{4} \qquad\qquad \tfrac{1}{2} \qquad\qquad 1\tfrac{3}{4}.$$

The rows are counted down the page, the first row being at the top.

> 3 (a) What does the $1\tfrac{3}{4}$ in the second row represent?
> (b) Write down the third row.

A *column* runs down the page and columns are counted from left to right. Thus the third column is

$$2\tfrac{1}{2}$$
$$1\tfrac{3}{4}$$
$$2\tfrac{1}{4}$$
$$2.$$

4 (a) What do the numbers in the third column represent?
(b) What number does the star * in the column

$$2$$
$$*$$
$$\tfrac{3}{4}$$
$$1 \qquad \text{stand for?}$$

(c) What information is given by this number *?
(d) Which column is this?

All the numerical information of a question appears in the rows and columns of such a table. When the rows and columns are brought together into one 'parcel' by a pair of square brackets like this,

$$\begin{bmatrix} 2 & 1\tfrac{1}{2} & 2\tfrac{1}{2} \\ 1\tfrac{1}{4} & \tfrac{1}{2} & 1\tfrac{3}{4} \\ \tfrac{3}{4} & 0 & 2\tfrac{1}{4} \\ 1 & 1 & 2 \end{bmatrix}$$

such a parcel is called a *matrix*. Capital letters are used to stand for *matrices* (note the plural). In printed work a bold or heavy type is used, for example, the matrix above might be denoted by **H**. In written work a wavy line is drawn underneath the capital letter. There are no special rules for choosing the letter for an information matrix. A possible reason for choosing **H** in this example might be that it stands for 'hours spent'!

When the numbers inside a matrix are data we have an *information matrix*. Another type of matrix, an instruction matrix, will be considered in Chapter 3.

For information matrices to be meaningful we must know the significance of the rows and the columns. For example, the third row of **H** represents 'Wednesday', the first column 'hours spent studying', and so on. In practice, having once stated them, we don't usually repeat these headings unless confusion is likely to arise.

The matrix **H** has 4 rows and 3 columns, and so we say that it is of *order* (or shape) 4×3. (This is read as, and sometimes written as, '4 by 3'.)

Any row of **H** may be considered as a matrix 'in its own right'. Thus

$$\mathbf{M} = [2 \quad 1\tfrac{1}{2} \quad 2\tfrac{1}{2}]$$

gives information for Monday. Such a matrix, with only one row, is sometimes called a *row matrix*. (It is also called a row vector.) Similarly

$$S = \begin{bmatrix} 2 \\ 1\frac{1}{4} \\ \frac{3}{4} \\ 1 \end{bmatrix}$$

may be called a *column matrix* (or column vector).

The individual numbers appearing in a matrix are called the *elements* of the matrix.

Exercise A

▷ 1 A factory produces three types of portable radios – Audio 1, Audio 2 and Audio 3. Audio 1 contains 1 transistor, 10 resistors and 5 capacitors. Audio 2 has 2 transistors, 18 resistors and 7 capacitors. Audio 3 has 3 transistors, 24 resistors and 10 capacitors. Express this information as a matrix.

▷ 2 The weekly purchases of three housewives are given in the table below.

	Butter (kg)	Sugar (kg)	Bacon (kg)	Bread (loaves)
Mrs A	$1\frac{1}{2}$	2	1	3
Mrs B	1	3	$1\frac{1}{2}$	4
Mrs C	2	1	2	5

(a) Write down the matrix **P** for these purchases.
(b) State the order of **P**.
(c) Write down Mrs C's purchases as a row matrix.
(d) Write down the purchases of sugar as a column matrix.

1.2 Route matrices

For the rest of this chapter we shall be considering two ways in which matrices can carry information about topological diagrams. In a topological diagram measurements such as length and angle are not accurate, but the links (*arcs*) between points (*nodes*) and the order of points on lines are reproduced correctly. The 'map' of the London Underground is a well-known topological diagram. In this chapter we shall think of the points as towns, and the links as the roads, or railway lines, joining these towns. (Further work on topology will be found in *Further Matrices and Transformations*.)

At present you may think of these applications as a separate topic, but later on you will find that this method of using matrices is the same in many apparently different situations. In fact, the matrix is one of those things that illustrate the underlying unity and symmetry of mathematics.

One-stage route matrices

Figure 2(a) shows the network of main railway lines linking four cities. From this you can see that, for example, there are two direct routes from London to Exeter. *Direct routes*, which run from one city to another without passing through a third city, are also called

4

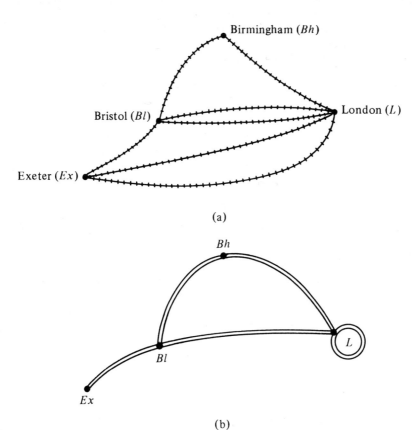

Birmingham (*Bh*)

Bristol (*Bl*)

London (*L*)

Exeter (*Ex*)

(a)

Bh

Bl

L

Ex

(b)

Figure 2

one-stage routes. The number of direct or one-stage routes between the cities in the network may be written in the form of a matrix. This is partially completed below.

$$
\begin{array}{c}
 & & \text{to} \\
 & & \begin{array}{cccc} Bh & Bl & Ex & L \end{array} \\
\text{from} & \begin{array}{c} Bh \\ Bl \\ Ex \\ L \end{array} & \left[\begin{array}{cccc} 0 & & & 1 \\ 1 & 0 & & \\ 0 & & & \\ & & 2 & \end{array}\right]
\end{array}
$$

Notice that we have chosen alphabetical order for the rows and columns. This is sensible, but not essential. But it is essential that the same order is used for rows as for columns.

1 (a) How many direct routes are there from Bristol to London, and from Exeter to Birmingham?

(b) Copy and complete the matrix for this network.

(c) What information is given by the zeros on the *leading diagonal* (the diagonal from top left to bottom right)?

6

Now look at Figure 2(b) which shows the network of motorways linking the same four cities. Notice that now, for example, the only one-stage route from Exeter is to Bristol.

2 (a) Do any of the cities have one-stage routes to all of the others?
(b) Does any city have a one-stage route to itself?
(c) Write down the matrix for this network.

3 Here is a matrix for the one-stage routes between four towns.

to

from		A	B	C	D
	A	0	2	0	1
	B	2	0	1	2
	C	0	1	2	0
	D	1	2	0	0

(a) Draw a network corresponding to this matrix.
(b) Is it possible to draw another network that is topologically different (for example, with a different number of roads joining two particular towns)?
(c) What is special about the shape of a route matrix?

If there are no one-way roads in a network, then the ways in which you can leave a town (from. . .) and the ways in which you can enter that town (to. . .) are the same. Thus any particular column of the route matrix will be the same as the corresponding row. For example, in the matrix for question **3** above we have

$$
\begin{bmatrix}
\cdot & 2 & \cdot & \cdot \\
2 & 0 & 1 & 2 \\
\cdot & 1 & \cdot & \cdot \\
\cdot & 2 & \cdot & \cdot
\end{bmatrix}
$$

Hence the matrix for such a network will be symmetrical about the leading diagonal.

Directed networks

A road along which the traffic is allowed to move in one direction only is called a *directed road* or *route*. An arrow shows the direction in which travel is allowed. A *directed network* is simply a network made up of directed routes.

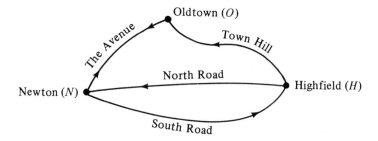

Figure 3

Figure 3 shows a directed network in which, for example, you can use North Road for travelling from Highfield to Newton, but not for travelling from Newton to Highfield. You may like to think of this network as being the bus routes that connect the suburbs of a large city.

> **4** (a) Copy and complete the matrix below to show the one-stage routes in the directed network of Figure 3.

$$
\begin{array}{c}
 & & \text{to} \\
 & & H \quad N \quad O \\
\text{from} \quad
\begin{array}{c} H \\ N \\ O \end{array}
&
\left[
\begin{array}{ccc}
0 & 1 & 1 \\
 & & \\
0 & &
\end{array}
\right]
\end{array}
$$

(b) What information is given by the third row of this matrix?
(c) What information is given by the second column?

Exercise B

> **1** Write down the route matrices for the networks in Figure 4. Note that when no arrow appears on a road in a directed network, that road is assumed to be two-way.

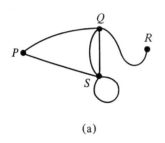 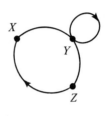

(a)   (b)

Figure 4

2 Draw networks corresponding to the matrices below.

(a)

$$
\begin{array}{c}
 & & \text{to} \\
 & & D \quad E \quad F \\
\text{from} \quad
\begin{array}{c} D \\ E \\ F \end{array}
&
\left[
\begin{array}{ccc}
0 & 0 & 1 \\
0 & 2 & 3 \\
1 & 3 & 4
\end{array}
\right]
\end{array}
$$

(b)

$$
\begin{array}{c}
 & & \text{to} \\
 & & K \quad L \quad M \\
\text{from} \quad
\begin{array}{c} K \\ L \\ M \end{array}
&
\left[
\begin{array}{ccc}
0 & 1 & 0 \\
0 & 2 & 1 \\
1 & 1 & 3
\end{array}
\right]
\end{array}
$$

3 (a) What type of numbers must the elements of a route matrix be?
(b) Explain why the elements on the leading diagonal of a non-directed route matrix are even numbers or zeros.

1.3 Two-stage route matrices

If, in the network in Figure 3, you are at Oldtown, it is not possible to travel directly to Highfield, but it is possible to go via Newton. A route that passes through one other town on its way is called a *two-stage route*. In this example the first stage is The Avenue and the second stage is South Road.

Consider all the possible two-stage routes starting from H. The first stage is either to O (via Town Hill) or to N (via North Road). From O there is only one possibility for the second stage, namely along The Avenue to N. But from N there are two possibilities for the second stage – either carry on to O along The Avenue, or return to H via South Road. Thus there is a total of three two-stage routes starting from H, one ending at O, one ending at N, and one ending back at H.

Check that the complete two-stage route matrix for the network in Figure 3 is

$$
\text{from}\quad
\begin{array}{c}
 \\
H \\
N \\
O
\end{array}
\begin{array}{c}
\text{to} \\
\begin{array}{ccc}
H & N & O
\end{array} \\
\left[
\begin{array}{ccc}
1 & 1 & 1 \\
0 & 2 & 1 \\
1 & 0 & 1
\end{array}
\right]
\end{array}
$$

It is more difficult to construct the two-stage route matrix for the network in Figure 1. To find, for example, all the routes starting from London it is helpful to draw a 'tree diagram' to show the various possibilities.

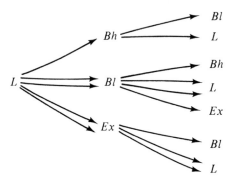

Figure 5

Note that as there are two ways of reaching Exeter on the first stage, there are two two-stage routes $L \to Ex \to Bl$.

How many two-stage routes are there from London to itself, via Exeter? To answer this, let the two lines from London to Exeter be called the Western (W) line, and the Southern (S) line. Figure 6 shows an expanded tree diagram for $L \to Ex \to L$.

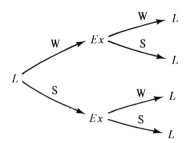

Figure 6

So we see that there are four two-stage routes $L \to Ex \to L$ in all.

▷ 1 (a) How many two-stage routes are there from London to itself via Bristol?
   (b) How many are there via Birmingham?
   (c) How many two-stage routes are there altogether from London to itself?

2 Draw tree diagrams similar to Figure 5 to show the two-stage routes from (a) Exeter, (b) Bristol, (c) Birmingham.

3   Write down the matrix to show all the two-stage routes for the network in Figure 1.

Consider the bus routes joining Alport and Highertown on the small island shown in Figure 7.

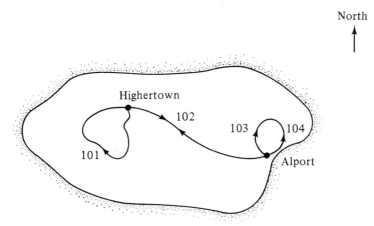

Figure 7

Route 101 is a circular local route in Highertown, running in a clockwise direction only. Route 102 runs both ways between Alport and Highertown. Lastly there is a circular route in Alport. When it runs in a clockwise direction it is route 103, and when it runs in an anti-clockwise direction it is route 104.

In this network, two-stage routes may be thought of as travelling on two buses. When it is possible, you are allowed to travel on the same route twice, thus a 103 followed by a 103 is a possible two-stage route from Alport to itself.

> **4**   (a) Describe, using the route numbers, the five two-stage routes from Alport to itself.
>   (b) Describe the two-stage routes from Highertown to itself.
>   (c) Describe the two-stage routes from Highertown to Alport.
>   (d) Complete the two-stage route matrix for this network.

Exercise C

> **1**   Construct the two-stage route matrix for the network shown in Figure 2(b).

> **2**   (a) Write down the one-stage route matrix for the directed network shown in Figure 8.

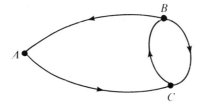

Figure 8

(b) List the two-stage routes in the form $A \to C \to B$.
(c) Construct the two-stage route matrix.

> **3**   Construct the two-stage route matrix for the network that you drew for question 3 of Section 1.2.

9

1.4 Incidence matrices

In the last section we looked at networks (thinking of them as topological maps) and considered a relation that had the departure towns (from. . .) as the domain and the arrival towns (to. . .) as the range.

In this section we are going to look at some other relations in a network, involving not only the towns but also the roads joining them, and the regions (or spaces) enclosed by the roads. For convenience we shall number the roads (1, 2, 3, . . .) and use small letters ($p, q, r, \ldots$) for the regions. We shall use Figure 9 as our network, and at this stage we shall consider only non-directed networks. Note that we include the outside as a region. It is a good practice to letter this regions first so that you don't forget it!

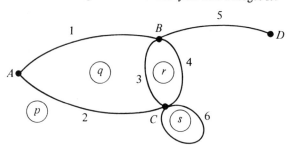

Figure 9

Town-on-road incidence matrix

This shows the relation between the towns (the domain) and the roads linking them (the range). The shape of the matrix will be

$$
\text{town} \quad
\begin{array}{c}
\\ A \\ B \\ C \\ D
\end{array}
\overset{\text{road}}{
\begin{array}{cccccc}
1 & 2 & 3 & 4 & 5 & 6 \\
\left[\begin{array}{cccccc}
& & & & & \\
& & & & & \\
& & & & & \\
& & & & &
\end{array} \right]
\end{array}}
$$

Town B is on (i.e. at the end of) roads 1, 3, 4 and 5 but it is not on roads 2 and 6, and so the row for B is [1 0 1 1 1 0]. We say that B is *incident* on roads 1, 3, 4 and 5. Similarly the row for C is [0 1 1 1 0 2]. As C is at both ends of road 6 (i.e. you can get onto road 6 from C in two ways) we put a 2 in the appropriate place in the matrix. (Some people prefer to think of incidence matrices as relation matrices which have only 0 and 1 as elements to indicate 'is not related' and 'is related', but this weakens the use and versatility of incidence matrices.)

 1 (a) Copy and complete the matrix above for the incidence of towns on roads.
   (b) Add up the numbers in each row. What information does this give about the towns?
   (c) Add up each column. What do you find?

Road-on-region incidence matrix

This matrix shows the incidence of roads on regions, that is, whether a road is part of the boundary of a region or not. For example, road 3 is incident on regions q and r, and road 1 is incident on regions p and q. As both sides of road 5 lead onto the region p we say that this road is doubly incident onto the region and the appropriate entry in the matrix will be a 2.

2 (a) Which is the domain of this matrix, and which the range?
   (b) State the order of this matrix.
   (c) Construct the matrix.
   (d) What is the sum of each row of this matrix?
   (e) What information is given by a column of this matrix?
   (f) What does the sum of the elements in the column for q tell you about the region q?

Town-on-region incidence matrix

Town A is incident on regions p and q because you can move directly from A into either of these regions. It is not incident on regions r and s.

3 (a) Is any town doubly incident on any region?
   (b) Construct the town-on-region incidence matrix.
   (c) What information is given by a column of this matrix, and the sum of the elements of a column?

We have thus compiled three of the incidence matrices for a given network. Sometimes, as in Exercise D below, the letters **R, S** and **T** are used for these three matrices as follows:

$$\mathbf{R} = \text{towns} \begin{bmatrix} \text{roads} \\ \ \end{bmatrix}, \quad \mathbf{S} = \text{roads} \begin{bmatrix} \text{regions} \\ \ \end{bmatrix}, \quad \mathbf{T} = \text{towns} \begin{bmatrix} \text{regions} \\ \ \end{bmatrix}.$$

arcs *node* *arcs* *regions* *nodes*

Exercise D

1 Construct the matrices **R, S** and **T** for the network in Figure 10.

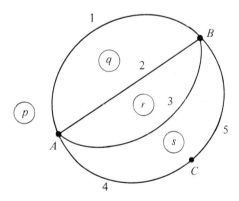

Figure 10

2 Draw possible networks corresponding to the following incidence matrices.

(a)
$$\mathbf{R} = \begin{array}{c} \\ D \\ E \\ F \end{array} \begin{array}{c} \begin{array}{ccccc} 1 & 2 & 3 & 4 & 5 \end{array} \\ \begin{bmatrix} 1 & 0 & 0 & 1 & 1 \\ 1 & 1 & 1 & 1 & 0 \\ 0 & 1 & 1 & 0 & 1 \end{bmatrix} \end{array}$$

(b)
$$\mathbf{S} = \begin{array}{c} \\ 1 \\ 2 \\ 3 \end{array} \begin{array}{c} \begin{array}{cc} m & n \end{array} \\ \begin{bmatrix} 1 & 1 \\ 1 & 1 \\ 1 & 1 \end{bmatrix} \end{array}$$

(c)
$$\mathbf{T} = \begin{array}{c} \\ X \\ Y \\ Z \end{array} \begin{array}{c} \begin{array}{cccc} p & q & r & s \end{array} \\ \begin{bmatrix} 1 & 1 & 1 & 0 \\ 1 & 2 & 1 & 1 \\ 0 & 1 & 0 & 1 \end{bmatrix} \end{array}$$

11

Summary

(1) A matrix is a rectangular array of numbers (the elements). It is denoted by a capital letter printed in bold.

$$A = \begin{bmatrix} 3 & 0 & 6 & {}^-2\frac{1}{2} \\ 2 & \frac{1}{2} & 10 & 1 \\ 5 & 1 & {}^-7 & {}^-4 \end{bmatrix}$$

(2) The matrix **A** above has 3 rows and 4 columns. It is of order (or shape) 3 × 4, or 3 by 4.

(3) A matrix with only one row, for example [4 0 3], is called a row matrix (or row vector). A matrix with only one column is called a column matrix (or column vector).

(4) A matrix that has the same number of rows as columns is called a square matrix. In

$$\begin{bmatrix} \mathbf{4} & 5 & {}^-6 \\ 2 & \mathbf{0} & 1 \\ 7 & {}^-8 & \mathbf{3} \end{bmatrix}$$

the elements printed in **bold** form the leading diagonal of the matrix.

(5) An information matrix contains information about the relation between the elements of a domain (listed at the side of the matrix) and the elements of a range (listed at the top).

The matrix		Won	Drawn	Lost
	Albion United	5	2	1
	Zorobo Town	1	4	3

shows the relation between the football teams (the domain) and the outcomes (the range) of their games.

(6) A route matrix is a (square) information matrix showing the number of routes between various towns in a network of roads. For a network with no one-way roads the matrix is symmetrical about the leading diagonal and each element of this diagonal is an even number or zero.

(7) A directed network has one or more one-way roads (for example, *AB, AC* and the loop at *C* in Figure 11).

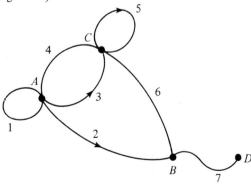

Figure 11

12

(8) The one-stage route matrix for the network in Figure 11 is

$$
\begin{array}{c}
 & \text{to} \\
 & \begin{array}{cccc} A & B & C & D \end{array} \\
\text{from} \quad \begin{array}{c} A \\ B \\ C \\ D \end{array} & \left[\begin{array}{cccc} 2 & 1 & 2 & 0 \\ 0 & 0 & 1 & 1 \\ 1 & 1 & 1 & 0 \\ 0 & 1 & 0 & 0 \end{array}\right].
\end{array}
$$

A one-stage route goes directly from one town to itself or to a second town without passing through any other town on its way.

(9) A two-stage route passes through one intermediate town on its way. The two-stage routes from C to B in Figure 11 are shown in Figure 12, and the full two-stage route matrix for Figure 11 is

$$
\begin{array}{c}
 & \text{to} \\
 & \begin{array}{cccc} A & B & C & D \end{array} \\
\text{from} \quad \begin{array}{c} A \\ B \\ C \\ D \end{array} & \left[\begin{array}{cccc} 6 & 4 & 7 & 1 \\ 1 & 2 & 1 & 0 \\ 3 & 2 & 4 & 1 \\ 0 & 0 & 1 & 1 \end{array}\right].
\end{array}
$$

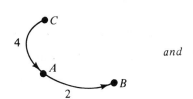

and

Figure 12

(10) The incidence matrices for a network show the relations between any two of towns, roads and regions. For example, the incidence matrix of towns on roads for the network in Figure 13 is

$$
\begin{array}{c}
 & \text{road} \\
 & \begin{array}{ccccc} 1 & 2 & 3 & 4 & 5 \end{array} \\
\text{town} \quad \begin{array}{c} A \\ B \\ C \\ D \end{array} & \left[\begin{array}{ccccc} 1 & 1 & 0 & 0 & 0 \\ 1 & 0 & 1 & 1 & 0 \\ 0 & 1 & 1 & 1 & 1 \\ 0 & 0 & 0 & 0 & 1 \end{array}\right]
\end{array}
$$

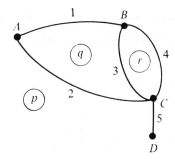

Figure 13

The usual incidence matrices are

$$\textbf{R} - \text{towns on roads,}$$
$$\textbf{S} - \text{roads on regions,}$$
$$\textbf{T} - \text{towns on regions.}$$

Post-test

1 In an athletics match the points for the individual events are: first place 4 points, second 2, and third 1. For the relay races the points are: first place 6, second 4, and third 2. Express this data as a 2 × 3 information matrix.

2 Write down the one-stage route matrices for each of the networks in Figure 14.

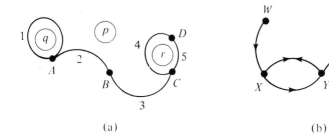

(a)   (b)   Figure 14

3 Write down the two-stage route matrices for each of the networks in Figure 14.

4 Draw networks for which the following are one-stage route matrices.

(a)

	to			
	A	B	C	D
A	0	0	1	2
B	0	2	0	1
C	1	0	0	0
D	2	1	0	2

from

(b)

	to		
	X	Y	Z
X	1	0	2
Y	2	0	3
Z	1	1	2

from

5 Construct the incidence matrices **R**, **S** and **T** for the network in Figure 14(a).

Assignment

1 Write down the one-stage route matrices for the networks in Figure 15 below.

2 Write down the two-stage route matrices for the networks in Figure 15 below.

3 (a) Draw a network corresponding to the one-stage route matrix

	to			
	G	H	J	K
G	0	1	0	1
H	1	0	1	0
J	0	1	0	1
K	1	1	1	0

from

(b) Is this matrix symmetrical about the leading diagonal? Explain your answer.

(c) Write down the two-stage matrix for this network.

4   Write down the **R, S** and **T** incidence matrices for each of the networks in Figure 15.

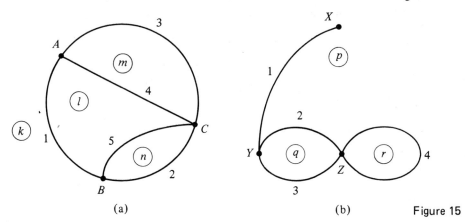

(a)   (b)   Figure 15

5   Draw a network corresponding to this incidence matrix.

road

		1	2	3	4
	A	0	1	0	0
town	B	1	1	1	0
	C	1	0	0	1
	D	0	0	1	1

Answers

Pre-test

1 Studying $2 + 1\frac{1}{4} + \frac{3}{4} + 1 = 5$ hours
TV $1\frac{1}{2} + \frac{1}{2} + 0 + 1 = 3$ hours
Travelling $2\frac{1}{2} + 1\frac{3}{4} + 2\frac{1}{4} + 2 = 8\frac{1}{2}$ hours

2 $4 \times £3.95 + 3 \times £7.75 + 8 \times £1.20 = £48.65$

3 (a) It is reasonable to assume that as you must pass through Swindon on the way to Swansea, Swindon is nearer to London.

(c) Yes   (e) Three

Parts (b) and (d) cannot be answered from the diagram.

1.1 Information tables

1   Points

West Ham	$9 \times 2 + 5 \times 1 + 6 \times 0 = 23$
Spurs	$6 \times 2 + 5 \times 1 + 8 \times 0 = 17$
Arsenal	$6 \times 2 + 4 \times 1 + 9 \times 0 = 16$
Chelsea	$3 \times 2 + 8 \times 1 + 8 \times 0 = 14$

2 1975 $2 \times 8p + \frac{1}{4} \times 64p + \frac{1}{10} \times 50p + 3 \times 6p = 55p$

1980 $2 \times 29p + \frac{1}{4} \times 144p + \frac{1}{10} \times 160p + 3 \times 17p = 161p$

3 (a) The $1\frac{3}{4}$ represents $1\frac{3}{4}$ hours spent on travelling on Tuesday.

(b) The third row is $\frac{3}{4}$ 0 $2\frac{1}{4}$.

4 (a) The numbers in the third column state the number of hours spent on travelling on each of the four days.

(b) ∗ stands for $1\frac{1}{4}$.

(c) This is the number of hours spent on study on Tuesday.

(d) It is the first column.

Exercise A

1

	T	R	C
Audio 1	1	10	5
Audio 2	2	18	7
Audio 3	3	24	10

$= N$

The information could be expressed in the form

	A1	A2	A3
T	1	2	3
R	10	18	24
C	5	7	10

Technically this is known as the *transpose* of **N**, and is written as **N'**.

    N shows the breakdown of the three types of radios, i.e. we are considering the radios as the domain. **N'** shows the distribution of the three types of components, with the components as the domain. Further work on domain and range will be found in Chapter 2 of *Algebra 1*.

2 (a)

	Butter (kg)	Sugar (kg)	Bacon (kg)	Bread (loaves)
Mrs A	$1\frac{1}{2}$	2	1	3
P = Mrs B	1	3	$1\frac{1}{2}$	4
Mrs C	2	1	2	5

(b) **P** is of order 3×4, as it has 3 rows and 4 columns.

(c) Mrs C [2   1   2   5]

(d)   Sugar (kg)

$$\begin{bmatrix} 2 \\ 3 \\ 1 \end{bmatrix}$$

1.2 Route matrices

1 (a) There are two direct routes from *Bl* to *L* and none from *Ex* to *Bh*.

(b)
                         to

		Bh	Bl	Ex	L
	Bh	0	1	0	1
from	Bl	1	0	1	2
	Ex	0	1	0	2
	L	1	2	2	0

(c) The zeros on the leading diagonal show that there are no 'circular' direct routes from a city to itself.

2 (a) Bristol is the only city linked directly to all the others.
   (b) London now has a one-stage route to itself.
   (c)

$$\begin{array}{c} & & \text{to} \\ & & \begin{array}{cccc} Bh & Bl & Ex & L \end{array} \\ \text{from} & \begin{array}{c} Bh \\ Bl \\ Ex \\ L \end{array} & \left[\begin{array}{cccc} 0 & 1 & 0 & 1 \\ 1 & 0 & 1 & 1 \\ 0 & 1 & 0 & 0 \\ 1 & 1 & 0 & 2 \end{array}\right] \end{array}$$

Notice the final 2. This means that you can leave London in two ways and end up back in London. These two ways are clockwise and anti-clockwise around the loop.

3 (a) See Figure A.

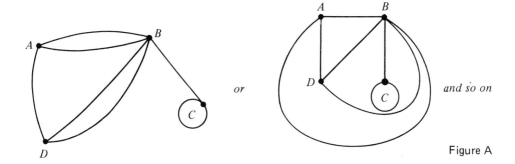

or   and so on

Figure A

   (b) No. The two examples given in Figure A may appear to be different, but they are topologically equivalent. For example, there are always five roads leading from B of which two go to A, one to C, and two to D.
   (c) A route matrix is always square in shape; that is, it has the same number of columns as rows.

4 (a)

$$\begin{array}{c} & & \text{to} \\ & & \begin{array}{ccc} H & N & O \end{array} \\ \text{from} & \begin{array}{c} H \\ N \\ O \end{array} & \left[\begin{array}{ccc} 0 & 1 & 1 \\ 1 & 0 & 1 \\ 0 & 1 & 0 \end{array}\right] \end{array}$$

   (b) The third row lists the ways in which you may *leave*, or depart from, Oldtown.
   (c) The second column lists the ways in which you may *enter*, or arrive in, Newton.
       Notice that the sum of the numbers in a row of a one-stage route matrix gives the total number of roads along which you may *leave* a particular town. The sum of a column gives the total along which you may *enter* a town. For a non-directed network these are, of course, the same for any one town.

Exercise B

1 (a)

	to			
	P	Q	R	S
from P	0	1	0	1
Q	1	0	1	2
R	0	1	0	0
S	1	2	0	2

(b)

	to		
	X	Y	Z
from X	0	1	0
Y	1	1	1
Z	1	1	0

2 (a) See Figure B. Notice that the total number of roads in the network is half the sum of the elements in the matrix, as each road appears twice in the matrix.

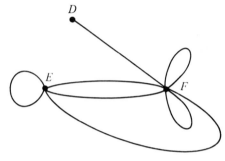

Figure B

(b) See Figure C. It is not essential to put arrows on two-way streets, although when drawing a directed network it is probably safer to do so. (Some people draw all the roads in a directed network as one-way roads, so that there would be nine roads for this question – but this can become unwieldy. For example there would be three loops at M!) On the other hand it is probably clearer (and less likely to lead to error when *interpreting* a directed network) if arrows are put only on the one-way roads.

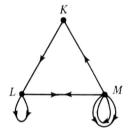

or

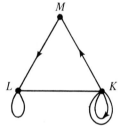

Figure C

3 (a) The elements must be non-negative integers.

(b) Any number on the leading diagonal shows the number of circular routes from that town to itself. In a non-directed network these must occur in pairs because for each loop it is possible to go round it either clockwise or anti-clockwise.

1.3 Two-stage route matrices

1 (a) 4, the same as $L \to Ex \to L$

(b) 1

(c) $4 + 4 + 1 = 9$

18

2 See Figure D.

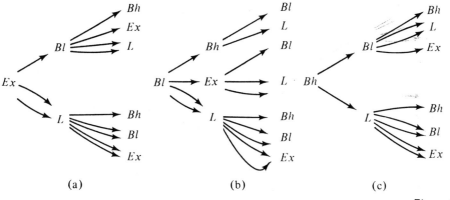

(a)   (b)   (c)

Figure D

3

	to			
from	*Bh*	*Bl*	*Ex*	*L*
Bh	2	2	3	2
Bl	2	6	4	3
Ex	3	4	5	2
L	2	3	2	9

4 (a) 102 west + 102 east, 103 + 103, 103 + 104, 104 + 103, 104 + 104
   (b) 101 + 101, 102 east + 102 west
   (c) 101 + 102, 102 + 103, 102 + 104
   (d)

	to	
from	*A*	*H*
A	5	3
H	3	2

Exercise C

1

	to			
from	*Bh*	*Bl*	*Ex*	*L*
Bh	2	1	1	3
Bl	1	3	0	3
Ex	1	0	1	1
L	3	3	1	6

The three routes from *Bh* to *L* are *Bh* → *Bl* → *L*, *Bh* → *L* (clockwise) → *L*, and *Bh* → *L* (anti-clockwise) → *L*.
The three routes from Bristol to itself are *Bl* → *Bh* → *Bl*, *Bl* → *Ex* → *Bl*, and *Bl* → *L* → *Bl*.
The six routes from London to itself are the four combinations obtained by going round the loop twice, *L* → *Bh* → *L*, and *L* → *Bl* → *L*.

19

2 (a)

$$
\begin{array}{c}
 & & \text{to} \\
 & & A \quad B \quad C \\
\text{from} \begin{array}{c} A \\ B \\ C \end{array} & \left[\begin{array}{ccc} 0 & 0 & 1 \\ 1 & 0 & 1 \\ 0 & 1 & 0 \end{array}\right]
\end{array}
$$

(b) $A \to C \to B$, $B \to A \to C$, $B \to C \to B$, $C \to B \to A$, $C \to B \to C$

(c)

$$
\begin{array}{c}
 & & \text{to} \\
 & & A \quad B \quad C \\
\text{from} \begin{array}{c} A \\ B \\ C \end{array} & \left[\begin{array}{ccc} 0 & 1 & 0 \\ 0 & 1 & 1 \\ 1 & 0 & 1 \end{array}\right]
\end{array}
$$

3

$$
\begin{array}{c}
 & & \text{to} \\
 & & A \quad B \quad C \quad D \\
\text{from} \begin{array}{c} A \\ B \\ C \\ D \end{array} & \left[\begin{array}{cccc} 5 & 2 & 2 & 4 \\ 2 & 9 & 2 & 2 \\ 2 & 2 & 5 & 2 \\ 4 & 2 & 2 & 5 \end{array}\right]
\end{array}
$$

If you completed this without missing any routes you are doing quite well! An easier method will be introduced in Chapter 2!

1.4 Incidence matrices

 1 (a)

$$
\begin{array}{c}
 & & \text{road} \\
 & & 1 \quad 2 \quad 3 \quad 4 \quad 5 \quad 6 \\
\text{town} \begin{array}{c} A \\ B \\ C \\ D \end{array} & \left[\begin{array}{cccccc} 1 & 1 & 0 & 0 & 0 & 0 \\ 1 & 0 & 1 & 1 & 1 & 0 \\ 0 & 1 & 1 & 1 & 0 & 2 \\ 0 & 0 & 0 & 0 & 1 & 0 \end{array}\right]
\end{array}
$$

(b) The sum of A's row is 2. There are two roads leaving A. Similarly sum(B) = 4, sum(C) = 5, and sum(D) = 1.
Notice that, by putting the 2 at the end of C's row, the sum gives the total number of exits from C.

(c) The sum of each column is 2, as each road has one town at each end.

 2 (a) The roads form the domain and the regions the range.

(b) The order of the matrix is 6 × 4.

(c)

$$
\begin{array}{c}
 & & \text{region} \\
 & & p \quad q \quad r \quad s \\
\text{road} \begin{array}{c} 1 \\ 2 \\ 3 \\ 4 \\ 5 \\ 6 \end{array} & \left[\begin{array}{cccc} 1 & 1 & 0 & 0 \\ 1 & 1 & 0 & 0 \\ 0 & 1 & 1 & 0 \\ 1 & 0 & 1 & 0 \\ 2 & 0 & 0 & 0 \\ 1 & 0 & 0 & 1 \end{array}\right]
\end{array}
$$

(d) The sum of each row is 2, as there is one region on either side of a road.

(e) A column tells us which roads make up the boundary of a particular region.

(f) The sum of q's column, 3, tells us that q is bounded by three roads.

3 (a) B and C are both doubly incident on p.

(b)

	region			
town	p	q	r	s
A	1	1	0	0
B	2	1	1	0
C	2	1	1	1
D	1	0	0	0

(c) A column states which towns are on the boundary of a particular region, and the sum of the column gives the number of towns that you would pass through in 'beating the bounds' of that region. The column sums in this matrix, therefore, will be the same as the column sums in the road-on-region matrix.

Exercise D

1

$$R = \begin{array}{c} \\ A \\ B \\ C \end{array} \begin{array}{ccccc} 1 & 2 & 3 & 4 & 5 \\ \left[\begin{array}{ccccc} 1 & 1 & 1 & 1 & 0 \\ 1 & 1 & 1 & 0 & 1 \\ 0 & 0 & 0 & 1 & 1 \end{array}\right] \end{array}, \quad S = \begin{array}{c} \\ 1 \\ 2 \\ 3 \\ 4 \\ 5 \end{array} \begin{array}{cccc} p & q & r & s \\ \left[\begin{array}{cccc} 1 & 1 & 0 & 0 \\ 0 & 1 & 1 & 0 \\ 0 & 0 & 1 & 1 \\ 1 & 0 & 0 & 1 \\ 1 & 0 & 0 & 1 \end{array}\right] \end{array}, \quad T = \begin{array}{c} \\ A \\ B \\ C \end{array} \begin{array}{cccc} p & q & r & s \\ \left[\begin{array}{cccc} 1 & 1 & 1 & 1 \\ 1 & 1 & 1 & 1 \\ 1 & 0 & 0 & 1 \end{array}\right] \end{array}$$

2 (a) See Figure E(a).

(b) See Figure E(b).

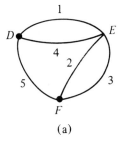
(a)

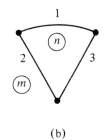
(b)

Figure E

(c) See Figure F. All the possible diagrams will be topologically equivalent (in three dimensions), but the matrix alone will not give the order of the regions around a particular town. It will, for example, tell us that from Y we can enter five possible sectors (two of which, in fact, are part of region q), but it will not tell us how these are situated in relation to each other.

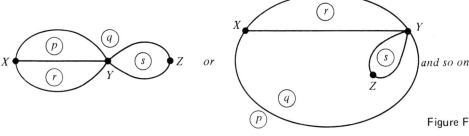

Figure F

Post-test

1

	place		
	first	second	third
individual event	4	2	1
relay race	6	4	2

2 (a)

		to		
from	A	B	C	D
A	2	1	0	0
B	1	0	1	0
C	0	1	0	2
D	0	0	2	0

(b)

		to		
from	W	X	Y	Z
W	0	1	0	0
X	0	0	2	0
Y	0	1	0	1
Z	0	0	0	0

3 (a)

		to		
from	A	B	C	D
A	5	2	1	0
B	2	2	0	2
C	1	0	5	0
D	0	2	0	4

(b)

		to		
from	W	X	Y	Z
W	0	0	2	0
X	0	2	0	2
Y	0	0	2	0
Z	0	0	0	0

4 (a) See Figure G(a).
(b) See Figure G(b).

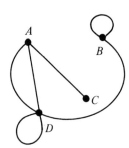

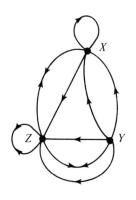

or

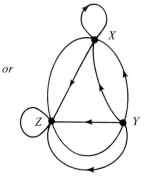

(a)   (b)   Figure G

5

$$R = \begin{matrix} & 1 & 2 & 3 & 4 & 5 \\ A & 2 & 1 & 0 & 0 & 0 \\ B & 0 & 1 & 1 & 0 & 0 \\ C & 0 & 0 & 1 & 1 & 1 \\ D & 0 & 0 & 0 & 1 & 1 \end{matrix}, \quad S = \begin{matrix} & p & q & r \\ 1 & 1 & 1 & 0 \\ 2 & 2 & 0 & 0 \\ 3 & 2 & 0 & 0 \\ 4 & 1 & 0 & 1 \\ 5 & 1 & 0 & 1 \end{matrix}, \quad T = \begin{matrix} & p & q & r \\ A & 2 & 1 & 0 \\ B & 2 & 0 & 0 \\ C & 2 & 0 & 1 \\ D & 1 & 0 & 1 \end{matrix}$$

22

2 Matrix algebra

Objectives

This is what you should be able to do after studying this chapter.
(1) Recognise when two matrices are compatible for addition and subtraction (that is, recognise whether it is possible to combine two matrices by addition or subtraction), and evaluate the sum or difference in such cases.
(2) Multiply a matrix by a scalar (a single number).
(3) Recognise when two matrices are compatible for multiplication, and evaluate the product in such cases.
(4) Apply the ideas of associativity and commutativity to matrix addition, and the idea of associativity to matrix multiplication, but recognise that in general matrix multiplication is not commutative.
(5) Recognise the appropriate identity matrices.
(6) Evaluate the determinant of a 2×2 matrix, and recognise when a 2×2 matrix is singular.
(7) Write down the inverse of any matrix under addition, and the inverse of a non-singular 2×2 matrix under multiplication.

Pre-test

> 1 Write down a matrix of order 3×3 that has zeros on its leading diagonal and ones elsewhere.

2 (a) In 1978 Anne bought six C60 cassettes, two C90s and one C120. In the same year Zoe bought three of each. Express this information as a 2×3 matrix.
   (b) Their purchases in 1980 are given in the matrix

$$
\begin{array}{c}
\\
\text{Anne} \\
\text{Zoe}
\end{array}
\begin{array}{ccc}
\text{C60} & \text{C90} & \text{C120} \\
\end{array}
\left[
\begin{array}{ccc}
5 & 0 & 7 \\
2 & 6 & 4
\end{array}
\right].
$$

How many C120s did Anne buy in 1980? How many C60s did Zoe buy?
   (c) Construct the matrix that shows their purchases for the two years put together.

3 In 1978 the people in question 2 bought their cassettes at the following prices – 45p for a C60, 70p for a C90 and 99p for a C120. Work out how much each person paid for their cassettes in 1978.

23

4 For the network shown in Figure 1, write down (a) the one-stage, and (b) the two-stage route matrix.

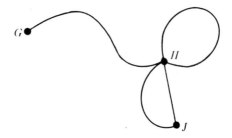

Figure 1

5 (a) Evaluate $15 + 2$, $2 + 15$, $15 - 2$ and $2 - 15$.
   (b) Evaluate 12×6, 6×12, $12 \div 6$ and $6 \div 12$.
   (c) Supply the missing word: These examples illustrate the fact that addition and multiplication are . . ., but subtraction and division are not . . .

6 (a) If P, Q, R are sets, is it *always* true that

$$(P \cap Q) \cap R = P \cap (Q \cap R)?$$

   (b) Is $(36 \div 6) \div 2 = 36 \div (6 \div 2)$?
   (c) Supply the missing word: Intersection of sets is . . ., but division of numbers is not . . .

2.1 Addition and subtraction

Matrix addition

This is a straightforward process and you have probably already used the ideas in answering question 2(c) of the pre-test. Set out as a matrix addition, the solution to that question is

	1978					1980					combined		
	C60	C90	C120			C60	C90	C120			C60	C90	C120
Anne	6	2	1	+		5	0	7	=		11	2	8
Zoe	3	3	3			2	6	4			5	9	7

From this we notice three things.
(a) To obtain an element of the sum we add the corresponding elements of the two matrices.
(b) This implies that the two matrices and the answer must all be of the same order. Thus it is not possible, for example, to add a 2×3 matrix to a 5×2 matrix. Such matrices are said to be *incompatible* for addition.
(c) Although it may be possible to add two matrices, it may not always be meaningful to do so. The 'sum' of

	C60	C90	C120
Anne	·	·	·
Zoe	·	·	·

and

	pages	photos	drawings
Book A	·	·	·
Book B	·	·	·

defies description!

24

Identity and inverse under addition

> 1 (a) Evaluate $\begin{bmatrix} 2 & 3 & {}^-1 \\ 0 & {}^-4 & 5 \end{bmatrix} + \begin{bmatrix} 0 & 0 & 0 \\ 0 & 0 & 0 \end{bmatrix}.$

(b) Evaluate $\begin{bmatrix} 1 & 0 & {}^-3 \\ 2 & {}^-4 & \frac{1}{2} \end{bmatrix} + \begin{bmatrix} {}^-1 & 0 & 3 \\ {}^-2 & 4 & {}^-\frac{1}{2} \end{bmatrix}.$

(c) What must be added to $\begin{bmatrix} 1 & {}^-2 \\ {}^-3 & 4 \end{bmatrix}$ to give an answer of $\begin{bmatrix} 0 & 0 \\ 0 & 0 \end{bmatrix}$?

In any algebra the *identity* for a particular operation is an element such that any other element is unchanged when combined with the identity. Thus, in the algebra of matrices, under the operation of addition,

the identity for the set of 3 × 2 matrices is $\begin{bmatrix} 0 & 0 \\ 0 & 0 \\ 0 & 0 \end{bmatrix}$,

that for the set of 2 × 4 matrices is $\begin{bmatrix} 0 & 0 & 0 & 0 \\ 0 & 0 & 0 & 0 \end{bmatrix}$,

and so on.

These matrices are also called *zero matrices*.

In any algebra the combination of an element and its *inverse* produces the identity element. Thus, under addition, the inverse of $\begin{bmatrix} 2 & 3 & {}^-1 \\ 0 & {}^-4 & 5 \end{bmatrix}$ is $\begin{bmatrix} {}^-2 & {}^-3 & 1 \\ 0 & 4 & {}^-5 \end{bmatrix}$

because $\begin{bmatrix} 2 & 3 & {}^-1 \\ 0 & {}^-4 & 5 \end{bmatrix} + \begin{bmatrix} {}^-2 & {}^-3 & 1 \\ 0 & 4 & {}^-5 \end{bmatrix} = \begin{bmatrix} 0 & 0 & 0 \\ 0 & 0 & 0 \end{bmatrix}.$

Associativity and commutativity

Let $A = \begin{bmatrix} 4 & 1 & 0 \\ {}^-2 & 3 & \frac{1}{2} \end{bmatrix}$, $B = \begin{bmatrix} {}^-7 & 6 & 1 \\ 1\frac{1}{2} & 0 & {}^-3 \end{bmatrix}$, $C = \begin{bmatrix} 0 & {}^-2 & 4 \\ {}^-3 & 9 & {}^-5 \end{bmatrix}.$

> 2 (a) Evaluate A + B, and then (A + B) + C.
   (b) Evaluate B + C, and then A + (B + C).

3 (a) Evaluate B + A and compare the answer with 2(a).
   (b) Evaluate C + B and compare the answer with 2(b).

The result of 2 suggests that matrix addition is associative, and the result of 3 that matrix addition is commutative. It is not difficult to see that whatever the elements, and whatever the order of the matrices, matrix addition is always associative and commutative.

Matrix subtraction

This is carried out in a similar way to addition.

> 4 Evaluate these. (a) $\begin{bmatrix} 2 & 0 & {}^-3 \\ {}^-1 & 2 & 7 \end{bmatrix} + \begin{bmatrix} 3 & 2 & 1 \\ {}^-1 & {}^-2 & {}^-3 \end{bmatrix}$

(b) $\begin{bmatrix} 5 & 2 & {}^-2 \\ {}^-2 & 0 & 4 \end{bmatrix} - \begin{bmatrix} 2 & 0 & {}^-3 \\ {}^-1 & 2 & 7 \end{bmatrix}$

(c) $\begin{bmatrix} 2 & ^-1 \\ 0 & 3 \end{bmatrix} - \begin{bmatrix} 0 & 0 \\ 0 & 0 \end{bmatrix}$

(d) $\begin{bmatrix} 0 & 0 \\ 0 & 0 \end{bmatrix} - \begin{bmatrix} 2 & ^-1 \\ 0 & 3 \end{bmatrix}$

Notice that the last two results show that matrix subtraction is not commutative, and they also suggest that there is no identity matrix under subtraction. Since matrix subtraction is very similar to 'ordinary' subtraction (of real numbers), it is in fact true that matrix subtraction is neither associative nor commutative, and does not possess an identity.

Multiplication by a scalar

A *scalar* is a single number. In the example below it is 4.

Check that if $D = \begin{bmatrix} 1 & ^-2 & 0 \\ 5 & 3 & ^-1 \end{bmatrix}$, then the sum $D + D + D + D$ is $\begin{bmatrix} 4 & ^-8 & 0 \\ 20 & 12 & ^-4 \end{bmatrix}$.

But $D + D + D + D = 4D$, hence $4D = \begin{bmatrix} 4 & ^-8 & 0 \\ 20 & 12 & ^-4 \end{bmatrix}$, that is

$$4\begin{bmatrix} 1 & ^-2 & 0 \\ 5 & 3 & ^-1 \end{bmatrix} = \begin{bmatrix} 4 & ^-8 & 0 \\ 20 & 12 & ^-4 \end{bmatrix}.$$

Thus to multiply a matrix by a scalar we multiply each element of the matrix by the scalar.

Exercise A

$$P = \begin{bmatrix} 1 & ^-2 \\ ^-3 & 0 \\ 7 & 1 \end{bmatrix}, \quad Q = \begin{bmatrix} 0 & 2 \\ 1 & ^-4 \\ 5 & ^-1 \end{bmatrix}, \quad R = \begin{bmatrix} 2 & ^-6 & 1 \\ 0 & 1 & ^-5 \end{bmatrix}$$

1 Evaluate these. (a) $P + Q$ (b) $P - Q$ (c) $3P$

2 Why is it not possible to work out $P + R$ or $Q - R$?

3 Write down the inverses, under addition, of (a) P, (b) R.

4 What is the identity, under matrix addition, for 3 × 5 matrices?

5 Evaluate these. (a) $Q + P$ (b) $Q - P$

2.2 Multiplication

In working out question 3 of the pre-test, all the information needed is in two matrices:

a purchase matrix $P = \begin{array}{c} \\ A \\ Z \end{array}\begin{bmatrix} \overset{C60}{6} & \overset{C90}{2} & \overset{C120}{1} \\ 3 & 3 & 3 \end{bmatrix}$,

and a cost matrix $Q_1 = \begin{array}{c} C60 \\ C90 \\ C120 \end{array}\begin{bmatrix} \overset{pence}{45} \\ 70 \\ 99 \end{bmatrix}$.

You should agree that the cost matrix is a column matrix, as the domain in this situation is {types of cassette}.

The question is: what type of combination of these two matrices will give us the answer that Anne spent 509 pence and Zoe spent 642 pence? Perhaps the first thing to do is to express the answer in matrix form. The domain is now {Anne, Zoe}, so the matrix will be

$$\begin{matrix} & \text{pence} \\ \text{Anne} & \begin{bmatrix} 509 \\ 642 \end{bmatrix} \\ \text{Zoe} & \end{matrix} = \mathbf{R}, \text{say.}$$

Now let us consider how we evaluate the figure of 509 pence for Anne.

$$509p = 6 \times 45p + 2 \times 70p + 1 \times 99p = (6 \times 45 + 2 \times 70 + 1 \times 99)p$$
(six cassettes at 45p each +. . .)

The 6, 2 and 1 come from the row matrix $\mathbf{A} = [6\ 2\ 1]$ – the top row of $\mathbf{P}$ – and the 45, 70 and 99 come from $\mathbf{Q_1}$. The figure 509 is obtained by a mixture of addition and multiplication of these elements. Clearly it is not an example of matrix addition (for one thing, the two matrices give different types of information). To avoid having to make up a new word for this operation, it is called *matrix multiplication*, and it is written as

$$\mathbf{A} \cdot \mathbf{Q_1} = \mathbf{R_a} \text{ (say)}$$

or

$$\mathbf{AQ_1} = \mathbf{R_a}$$

that is, $[6\ 2\ 1] \begin{bmatrix} 45 \\ 70 \\ 99 \end{bmatrix} = [509].$

This follows the usual convention that multiplication may be expressed by a dot, or by no symbol at all. Note, however, that although we use the word 'multiplication', this operation – unlike matrix addition – involves more than the corresponding operation for real numbers.

We have expressed all our matrices so that the members of the domain are listed at the side of the matrix. It follows, therefore, that one of the things that we can do under matrix multiplication is to combine a row matrix with a column matrix to give a 1 × 1 matrix (a matrix with a single element) as the product.

> 1 (a) State a condition on the number of elements if a row matrix $\mathbf{X}$ and a column matrix $\mathbf{Y}$ are to be compatible for multiplication.
   (b) State a condition for the product of two matrices to be meaningful.
   (c) Express the cost to Zoe in 1978 as the product of two matrices $\mathbf{Z}$ and $\mathbf{Q_1}$. Call this $\mathbf{R_z}$ and evaluate $\mathbf{R_z}$.

2 The prices of cassettes in 1980 were

$$\begin{matrix} & \text{pence} \\ \text{C60} & \begin{bmatrix} 60 \\ 89 \\ 115 \end{bmatrix} \\ \text{C90} & \\ \text{C120} & \end{matrix} .$$

(a) Using the data in question 2(b) of the pre-test, write down, and evaluate, a suitable product of two matrices to find out how much Anne spent in 1980.
(b) Do the same for Zoe.

So far we have evaluated the two elements of **R** separately:

$$[6 \ 2 \ 1] \begin{bmatrix} 45 \\ 70 \\ 99 \end{bmatrix} = [509] \quad \text{and} \quad [3 \ 3 \ 3] \begin{bmatrix} 45 \\ 70 \\ 99 \end{bmatrix} = [642].$$

In each case the working is similar, and the matrix Q_1 is used both times, and so it is useful in written work to combine these two parts as follows:

$$\begin{bmatrix} 6 & 2 & 1 \\ 3 & 3 & 3 \end{bmatrix} \begin{bmatrix} 45 \\ 70 \\ 99 \end{bmatrix} = \begin{bmatrix} 509 \\ 642 \end{bmatrix}$$

that is, $P \cdot Q_1 = R$.

This is similar to saying that

$$\text{if } 5x = p \quad \text{and} \quad 8x = q, \quad \text{then} \quad (5+8)x = (p+q).$$

It is a shorter way of writing down the information and the answer – but we still have to do the same amount of arithmetic!

 3   Rewrite question **2** above in a similar way.

4   Suppose that in 1979 Anne and Zoe bought the same *selection* of cassettes as they did in 1978, but that the prices had been increased to 52p, 79p and 105p respectively.
(a) Express the new prices as a 3×1 matrix Q_2.
(b) Write down the appropriate single matrix product that will give each person's total cost in 1979.
(c) Call the product of these two matrices **S**, and evaluate **S**.

This last calculation $(P \cdot Q_2)$ is very similar to the earlier calculation of $P \cdot Q_1$. So it is logical to take the 'shorthand' a final stage, and combine $P \cdot Q_1 = R$ with $P \cdot Q_2 = S$ to give

				1978	1979			1978	1979
Anne	6	2	1	45	52	= Anne	509	575
Zoe	3	3	3	70	79	Zoe	642	708
				99	105			

The basic rule is still the same. To find a particular element of the product, the correspond-ing row of the first matrix has to be combined with the appropriate column of the second matrix by the method used above.

As this is an unfamiliar operation it will be worth looking at another example.

The matrix **C** below shows how many Christmas cards a family send each year by 1st class and 2nd class post. The matrix **P** gives the postage rates for the two classes for three selected years. We can combine these to find the cost to each person in each of the three years, because a combination of

'persons → classes' with 'classes → years'

gives   'persons → years'.

	1st	2nd
Mr N	30	12
Mrs N	6	11
Mary	4	28
Mark	8	19

C multiplied by P = T

$$
\begin{array}{c}
 \\
\text{Mr N} \\
\text{Mrs N} \\
\text{Mary} \\
\text{Mark}
\end{array}
\begin{array}{cc}
\text{1st} & \text{2nd} \\
\left[\begin{array}{cc}
30 & 12 \\
6 & 11 \\
4 & 28 \\
8 & 19
\end{array}\right.
\end{array}
\quad
\begin{array}{c}
 \\
\text{1st} \\
\text{2nd}
\end{array}
\begin{array}{ccc}
1973 & 1976 & 1979 \\
3\frac{1}{2} & 8\frac{1}{2} & 10 \\
3 & 6\frac{1}{2} & 8
\end{array}
\quad = \quad
\begin{array}{c}
 \\
\text{Mr N} \\
\text{Mrs N} \\
\text{Mary} \\
\text{Mark}
\end{array}
\begin{array}{ccc}
1973 & 1976 & 1979 \\
\cdot & \cdot & \cdot \\
\cdot & x & \cdot \\
\cdot & \cdot & y \\
\cdot & \cdot & \cdot
\end{array}
$$

To work out, for example, the value of x we note that it is the cost to *Mrs N* in *1976*. So we combine *Mrs N's row* with the *1976 column*

$$
\begin{bmatrix}
\cdot & \cdot \\
6 & 11 \\
\cdot & \cdot \\
\cdot & \cdot
\end{bmatrix}
\begin{bmatrix}
\cdot & 8\frac{1}{2} & \cdot \\
\cdot & 6\frac{1}{2} & \cdot
\end{bmatrix}
=
\begin{bmatrix}
\cdot & \cdot & \cdot \\
\cdot & x & \cdot \\
\cdot & \cdot & \cdot \\
\cdot & \cdot & \cdot
\end{bmatrix}
$$

to give $6 \times 8\frac{1}{2} + 11 \times 6\frac{1}{2} = 122\frac{1}{2}$ as the value of x
(i.e. six 1st class at $8\frac{1}{2}$p each + eleven 2nd class at $6\frac{1}{2}$p each).

> 5 (a) Which row and which column are combined to give the value of y? Verify that $y = 264$.
  (b) Evaluate the remaining elements of **T**.

▶8

Exercise B

> 1 Inland Air has a fleet of 13 passenger aircraft: 4 Dragons, 2 Jabberwocks and 7 Unicorns. Go-Air has a fleet of 10: 1 Dragon, 3 Jabberwocks and 6 Unicorns. A Dragon can carry 9 'luxury' passengers and 24 'economy' passengers, a Jabberwock can carry 12 of each, and a Unicorn carries 32 'economy' passengers only.
  (a) Express the numbers of aircraft as a 2 × 3 matrix **N**.
  (b) Express the seating capacity of the planes as a 3 × 2 matrix **S**.
  (c) Verify that Inland Air can carry a maximum of 344 'economy' passengers.
  (d) What is the maximum number of 'luxury' passengers that Go-Air can carry?
  (e) Evaluate the matrix **T = N . S**.
  (f) What information is given by **T**?

▶9

> 2 Evaluate the following matrix products.

(a) $\begin{bmatrix} 1 & ^-2 & 7 \\ 0 & 3 & 4 \end{bmatrix} \begin{bmatrix} 1 \\ 2 \\ 3 \end{bmatrix}$

(b) $\begin{bmatrix} 2 & 4 & 6 \end{bmatrix} \begin{bmatrix} 9 & ^-7 \\ ^-5 & 3 \\ 1 & ^-1 \end{bmatrix}$

(c) $\begin{bmatrix} ^-6 & 2 \\ 3 & ^-1 \end{bmatrix} \begin{bmatrix} 2 & 3 \\ 4 & 5 \end{bmatrix}$

▶10

2.3 Properties of matrix multiplication

Compatibility

 1 Which of the following is it possible to evaluate?

(a) $[1 \ 2 \ 3] \begin{bmatrix} 4 \\ 5 \end{bmatrix}$
    (b) $[1 \ 2] \begin{bmatrix} 3 \\ 4 \end{bmatrix}$
    (c) $\begin{bmatrix} 1 \\ 2 \end{bmatrix} \begin{bmatrix} 3 \\ 4 \end{bmatrix}$

(d) $\begin{bmatrix} 1 \\ 2 \end{bmatrix} [3 \ 4]$
    (e) $[1 \ 2] \begin{bmatrix} 3 \\ 4 \\ 5 \end{bmatrix}$
    (f) $\begin{bmatrix} 1 \\ 2 \end{bmatrix} [3 \ 4 \ 5]$

2 For which of the following is it possible to evaluate the matrix product **X . Y**? Where it is possible, state the order (shape) of the product.

	order of **X**	order of **Y**
(a)	3×2	2×7
(b)	5×3	5×4
(c)	3×6	7×3
(d)	2×4	4×5
(e)	2×2	2×2
(f)	3×4	4×3

These two questions will remind you that, for matrix multiplication to be possible, the number of elements in a row of the first matrix must equal the number of elements in a column of the second. In other words, the number of columns of the first matrix **X** must equal the number of rows of the second matrix **Y**, as for example in 2(d) above where **X** has 4 columns and **Y** has 4 rows.

If we enclose these 'shapes' in round brackets, and place them side by side

$$(2 \times 4) . (4 \times 5)$$

we see a similarity with two dominoes, and so this rule for compatibility is sometimes called the 'domino rule'. Notice also that the outer numbers of the 'dominoes' give the shape of the product

$$(2 \times 4) . (4 \times 5) \rightarrow (2 \times 5).$$

Commutativity

 3 Let $A = \begin{bmatrix} 1 & {}^-2 \\ 5 & 4 \end{bmatrix}$ and $B = \begin{bmatrix} {}^-1 & 0 \\ 3 & 8 \end{bmatrix}$.

(a) Why is it possible to evaluate both **A . B** and **B . A**?
(b) Evaluate these two products and compare the results.

For an operation to possess a property such as commutativity, the property must be true for all possible members of the set. One counter-example, as in **3** above, is sufficient for the operation to be classified as 'non-commutative'. Thus we see that matrix multiplication is non-commutative. (This is not to say that the product of two particular matrices is never commutative. We shall meet some examples later – they are sometimes referred to as commutative pairs.)

It is not, therefore, always sufficient to say 'find the product of **A** and **B**'. Hence, if we

30

want the product **A** . **B**, we can say either *'pre-multiply* the matrix **B** by **A**' or *'post-multiply* **A** by **B**'. Similarly, **B** . **A** is the result of pre-multiplying **A** by **B**. (The prefix *pre-* means 'in front of', and *post-* means 'after' or 'behind'.)

Associativity

> 4 Let A and B be as in question 3, and let $C = \begin{bmatrix} 2 & -3 \\ 1 & 0 \end{bmatrix}$.

    (a) Evaluate (**A** . **B**) . **C**, **B** . **C** and **A** . (**B** . **C**).

    (b) Evaluate **C** . (**A** . **B**) and (**B** . **C**) . **A** and compare your answers with the previous results.

These results suggest that matrix multiplication is associative even though it is not commutative. Hence it is possible to write an 'extended' product such as **B** . **A** . **C** without brackets, and without ambiguity. Question 4 shows that we shall obtain the same answer whether we work this out as **B** . **A** and then (**B** . **A**) . **C**, or as **A** . **C** and then **B** . (**A** . **C**), provided we keep to the order **B-A-C**.

Exercise C

$$P = \begin{bmatrix} 1 & 0 \\ 2 & -3 \end{bmatrix}, \qquad Q = \begin{bmatrix} 1 & -1 & 1 \\ -2 & 1 & 0 \end{bmatrix}, \qquad R = \begin{bmatrix} 3 & -2 \\ 0 & 1 \\ -1 & 4 \end{bmatrix}$$

> 1 Use the domino rule to find which of the following can be evaluated, and write down the order of those products that are possible.
    (a) **P** . **Q**   (b) **P** . **R**   (c) **Q** . **P**   (d) **Q** . **R**   (e) **R** . **P**   (f) **R** . **Q**

  2 Which two results from question 1 show that matrix multiplication is obviously not commutative?

  3 Evaluate those products in question 1 that are possible.

2.4 Identity and inverse of 2 × 2 matrices

Identity

> 1 $X = \begin{bmatrix} 5 & -2 \\ -4 & 3 \end{bmatrix}$.

    Evaluate the products **X** . **Y** and **Y** . **X** when **Y** is as follows.

    (a) $\begin{bmatrix} 1 & 1 \\ 1 & 1 \end{bmatrix}$ (b) $\begin{bmatrix} 1 & 1 \\ 0 & 0 \end{bmatrix}$ (c) $\begin{bmatrix} 1 & 0 \\ 0 & 1 \end{bmatrix}$ (d) $\begin{bmatrix} 0 & 1 \\ 1 & 0 \end{bmatrix}$ (e) $\begin{bmatrix} 0 & 1 \\ 0 & 1 \end{bmatrix}$

    (f) $\begin{bmatrix} 1 & 0 \\ 0 & 0 \end{bmatrix}$ (g) $\begin{bmatrix} 0 & 1 \\ 1 & 1 \end{bmatrix}$

From the above results we can see that for the set of 2 × 2 matrices under multiplication the identity matrix is $\begin{bmatrix} 1 & 0 \\ 0 & 1 \end{bmatrix}$.

This is sometimes called the *unit matrix* (of order 2 × 2) and is denoted by $\mathbf{I}$ (or $\mathbf{I_2}$). It has the usual property, namely that for any 2 × 2 matrix $\mathbf{X}$,

$$\mathbf{I \cdot X = X \cdot I = X}.$$

Inverse

For any given matrix $\mathbf{X}$ can we find a matrix $\mathbf{Y}$ such that $\mathbf{X \cdot Y = Y \cdot X = I}$ (i.e. such that $\mathbf{X}$ and $\mathbf{Y}$ are a commutative pair whose product is the identity matrix)?

  2 If $\mathbf{X} = \begin{bmatrix} 2 & 1 \\ 5 & 3 \end{bmatrix}$, evaluate $\mathbf{X \cdot Y}$ and $\mathbf{Y \cdot X}$ when $\mathbf{Y}$ is as follows.

(a) $\begin{bmatrix} 2 & 1 \\ 5 & 3 \end{bmatrix}$　　　　(b) $\begin{bmatrix} 3 & ^-1 \\ ^-5 & 2 \end{bmatrix}$

3 If $\mathbf{X} = \begin{bmatrix} 5 & 1 \\ 8 & 2 \end{bmatrix}$, evaluate $\mathbf{X \cdot Y}$ and $\mathbf{Y \cdot X}$ when $\mathbf{Y}$ is as follows.

(a) $\begin{bmatrix} 2 & ^-1 \\ ^-8 & 5 \end{bmatrix}$　(b) $\begin{bmatrix} 4 & ^-2 \\ ^-16 & 10 \end{bmatrix}$　(c) $\begin{bmatrix} 1 & ^-\frac{1}{2} \\ ^-4 & 2\frac{1}{2} \end{bmatrix}$

4 Evaluate these.

(a) $\begin{bmatrix} 8 & ^-3 \\ ^-4 & 2 \end{bmatrix}\begin{bmatrix} 2 & 3 \\ 4 & 8 \end{bmatrix}$ (b) $\begin{bmatrix} 2 & ^-3 \\ 4 & 1 \end{bmatrix}\begin{bmatrix} 1 & 3 \\ ^-4 & 2 \end{bmatrix}$ (c) $\begin{bmatrix} 1 & 2 \\ 3 & 4 \end{bmatrix}\begin{bmatrix} 4 & ^-2 \\ ^-3 & 1 \end{bmatrix}$

From these results we see that the pair of matrices $\begin{bmatrix} a & b \\ c & d \end{bmatrix}$ and $\begin{bmatrix} d & ^-b \\ ^-c & a \end{bmatrix}$ are

commutative under multiplication, giving the product $\begin{bmatrix} n & 0 \\ 0 & n \end{bmatrix}$, where $n = a \times d - b \times c$.

So if we want to end up with the matrix $\begin{bmatrix} 1 & 0 \\ 0 & 1 \end{bmatrix}$, all the elements of the second

matrix must be divided by n. Thus the inverse of $\mathbf{X} = \begin{bmatrix} a & b \\ c & d \end{bmatrix}$ is

$$\frac{1}{n}\begin{bmatrix} d & ^-b \\ ^-c & a \end{bmatrix} \quad \text{or} \quad \begin{bmatrix} \dfrac{d}{n} & \dfrac{^-b}{n} \\ \dfrac{^-c}{n} & \dfrac{a}{n} \end{bmatrix}$$

To show that this matrix has a special connection with $\mathbf{X}$ it is denoted by $\mathbf{X}^{-1}$.

The number $n = ad - bc$ is called the *determinant* of the matrix. The symbol Δ (*delta* - a capital letter from the Greek alphabet) is often used for the determinant. If $\Delta = 0$, the matrix has no inverse and is said to be *singular*.

  5 Where possible, write down the inverses of these matrices.

(a) $\begin{bmatrix} 8 & ^-3 \\ ^-4 & 2 \end{bmatrix}$　(b) $\begin{bmatrix} 2 & ^-3 \\ 4 & 1 \end{bmatrix}$　(c) $\begin{bmatrix} 1 & 2 \\ 3 & 4 \end{bmatrix}$　(d) $\begin{bmatrix} 2 & ^-3 \\ ^-4 & 6 \end{bmatrix}$

To summarise, the stages in finding the inverse of the 2×2 matrix $\begin{bmatrix} a & b \\ c & d \end{bmatrix}$ are as follows.

(a) Evaluate the determinant $\Delta = ad - bc$. If this is zero - stop! There is no inverse.
(b) If $\Delta \neq 0$, change over the a and d elements.
(c) Change the sign (+ or −) in front of the b and c elements.
(d) Divide each element by Δ.

Exercise D

> 1   Write down, where possible, the inverses of the following.

(a) $\begin{bmatrix} 2 & 1 \\ 5 & 3 \end{bmatrix}$ (b) $\begin{bmatrix} 7 & -5 \\ -4 & 3 \end{bmatrix}$ (c) $\begin{bmatrix} 5 & 2 \\ -1 & 0 \end{bmatrix}$ (d) $\begin{bmatrix} -3 & 6 \\ -4 & 8 \end{bmatrix}$

(e) $\begin{bmatrix} 4 & 12 \\ 3 & 8 \end{bmatrix}$ (f) $\begin{bmatrix} -3 & 5 \\ 2 & -3 \end{bmatrix}$ (g) $\begin{bmatrix} -3 & -5 \\ 7 & 11 \end{bmatrix}$ (h) $\begin{bmatrix} 3 & -2 \\ 1 & 1 \end{bmatrix}$

> 2   What do you think is the identity, I_3, for 3×3 matrices under multiplication?

Confirm your answer by multiplying it by the matrix $\mathbf{Q} = \begin{bmatrix} 1 & 0 & -2 \\ 2 & -1 & 3 \\ 4 & 6 & 0 \end{bmatrix}$.

3   $\mathbf{A} = \begin{bmatrix} 2 & 0 & -2 \\ 0 & 0 & 1 \\ -2 & -4 & 3 \end{bmatrix}$ and $\mathbf{B} = \begin{bmatrix} 2 & 4 & 0 \\ -1 & 1 & -1 \\ 0 & 4 & 0 \end{bmatrix}$.

(a) Evaluate $\mathbf{A} \cdot \mathbf{B}$.   (b) Write down $\mathbf{A}^{-1}$, the inverse of $\mathbf{A}$ under multiplication.
(c) Write down the inverse of $\mathbf{B}$.

2.5 Applications of matrix multiplication

The examples in this chapter involving labelled information matrices have shown some applications of this operation of matrix multiplication. You may also by now have realised that the quicker way to obtain a two-stage route matrix is to square the corresponding one-stage route matrix (i.e. to multiply it by itself). This idea, and the combination of incidence matrices, will be considered more fully in *Further Matrices and Transformations*.

The solution of simultaneous linear equations may be obtained by matrix methods. This is also covered in *Further Matrices and Transformations*. Historically, matrices were developed for the solution of more complicated simultaneous equations.

A somewhat less expected use of matrices is in the algebraic treatment of transformation geometry. The remainder of this book covers this work.

A final note

There are a number of occasions in matrix work when the order 'rows first, columns second' is used. Two such are the describing of the order (shape) of a matrix, and in finding the product of one matrix with a second. A useful way of remember this is the mnemonic RC (for Roman Catholic). It can be said that matrices are very catholic in the occasions in which they may be used!

Summary

(1) Two matrices are compatible for addition and subtraction (that is, it is possible to combine them by these methods) when they are of the same order.

(2) *Matrix addition.*

$$\begin{bmatrix} 1 & 2 \\ ^-4 & 0 \\ 9 & ^-\tfrac{1}{2} \end{bmatrix} + \begin{bmatrix} ^-3 & 5 \\ ^-1 & 6 \\ ^-8 & \tfrac{1}{2} \end{bmatrix} = \begin{bmatrix} ^-2 & 7 \\ ^-5 & 6 \\ 1 & 0 \end{bmatrix}$$

Matrix addition is associative and commutative.

(3) *Multiplication by a scalar*

$$3 \begin{bmatrix} 0 & 4 & ^-2 \\ \tfrac{1}{2} & ^-3 & 1 \end{bmatrix} = \begin{bmatrix} 0 & 12 & ^-6 \\ 1\tfrac{1}{2} & ^-9 & 3 \end{bmatrix}$$

(4) Two matrices are compatible for matrix multiplication when they follow the 'domino rule': the number of columns in the first matrix must be equal to the number of rows in the second. For example,

$$\underset{(2 \times 3)\,(3 \times 5)}{\mathbf{A} \cdot \mathbf{B}} = \underset{(2 \times 5)}{\mathbf{C}}$$

These two numbers
must be the same.

The outer numbers of the 'dominoes' for **A** and **B** give the 'domino', or order, of **C**.

(5) *Matrix multiplication.* Each element of the product is a 'marrying' or combination of a complete *row* of the first matrix with a complete *column* of the second.

$$\underset{\mathbf{A}}{\begin{bmatrix} \cdot & \cdot & \cdot \\ 2 & 3 & 4 \end{bmatrix}} \underset{\mathbf{B}}{\begin{bmatrix} \cdot & \cdot & 6 & \cdot & \cdot \\ \cdot & \cdot & ^-5 & \cdot & \cdot \\ \cdot & \cdot & 1 & \cdot & \cdot \end{bmatrix}} = \underset{\mathbf{C}}{\begin{bmatrix} \cdot & \cdot & \cdot & \cdot & \cdot \\ \cdot & \cdot & 1 & \cdot & \cdot \end{bmatrix}}$$

In this example, the second row of **A** is combined with the third column of **B** to give the *element* in the second row and third column of **C**, following the method $2 \times 6 + 3 \times {}^-5 + 4 \times 1 = 1$. Matrix multiplication may be indicated by a dot, or by no symbol at all (compare this with xy which means x multiplied by y). Matrix multiplication is associative, but in general it is not commutative.

(6) The operation of division does not exist in matrix algebra.

(7) *Identity matrices.* Under addition and subtraction, the identity is a *zero* matrix, all of whose elements are zeros. Under multiplication, the identity of a set of square matrices of order $n \times n$ is the *unit* matrix of order $n \times n$, which has 1s on its leading diagonal and zeros elsewhere. For example,

$$\begin{bmatrix} 0 & 0 & 0 \\ 0 & 0 & 0 \end{bmatrix}$$ is the zero matrix for 2×3 matrices under addition, and

$$\begin{bmatrix} 1 & 0 & 0 \\ 0 & 1 & 0 \\ 0 & 0 & 1 \end{bmatrix}$$ is the unit matrix for 3×3 matrices under multiplication.

(8) The determinant of the 2×2 matrix $\begin{bmatrix} a & b \\ c & d \end{bmatrix}$ is $\Delta = ad - bc$. If $\Delta = 0$, the matrix is said to be singular.

(9) *The inverse of a matrix*. Under addition, the inverse of $\begin{bmatrix} p & q & r \\ s & t & u \end{bmatrix}$ is $\begin{bmatrix} {}^-p & {}^-q & {}^-r \\ {}^-s & {}^-t & {}^-u \end{bmatrix}$.

Under multiplication, the inverse of a non-singular 2×2 matrix $\begin{bmatrix} a & b \\ c & d \end{bmatrix}$ is

$$\frac{1}{\Delta} \begin{bmatrix} d & {}^-b \\ {}^-c & a \end{bmatrix}, \text{ or } \begin{bmatrix} \dfrac{d}{\Delta} & \dfrac{{}^-b}{\Delta} \\ \dfrac{{}^-c}{\Delta} & \dfrac{a}{\Delta} \end{bmatrix}.$$

A singular matrix does not have an inverse under multiplication. The combination of a matrix and its inverse is the identity matrix.

(10) The mnemonic 'RC', implying 'row first, column second', is useful in matrix work.

Post-test

$$D = \begin{bmatrix} 1 & 5 \\ 0 & {}^-2 \end{bmatrix}, \quad E = \begin{bmatrix} 4 & 3 \\ {}^-2 & {}^-1\frac{1}{2} \end{bmatrix}, \quad F = \begin{bmatrix} {}^-2 & 0 & 1 \\ 3 & 4 & 2 \end{bmatrix}$$

> 1   List five ways in which the matrix **D** may be combined with the matrix **E**, and find the result in each case.

2   (a) Evaluate D^2 ($= D \cdot D$).
     (b) Evaluate 4**E**.
     (c) Which combination of **E** and **F** is compatible for multiplication? Evaluate this combination.
     (d) Why is it not possible to evaluate F^2?

3   (a) What is the identity, under addition, of the set of matrices of which **F** is a member?
     (b) Write down the inverse under addition of **F**.

4   (a) Evaluate the determinants of **D** and **E**.
     (b) Which of these two is a singular matrix?
     (c) Write down the inverse under multiplication of the other.

Assignment

1   The Wedgwood booklet of stamps issued in 1980 contains four panes (pages) of stamps. Pane A has nine 12p stamps, pane B has nine 10p stamps, pane C has six 2p stamps, and pane D has four 12p + four 10p + one 2p stamps.
     (a) Express this information in a 4×3 matrix **S** with the column headings in the order 2p 10p 12p.
     (b) Pre-multiply **S** by the matrix $N = \begin{bmatrix} 1 & 1 & 1 & 1 \end{bmatrix}$ (that is, evaluate $N \cdot S$). What information does this product give?
     (c) Post-multiply **S** by the matrix $P = \begin{bmatrix} 2 \\ 10 \\ 12 \end{bmatrix}$.
     What information does this product give?
     (d) Evaluate $N \cdot S \cdot P$.

2 The one-stage route matrix for a network is

$$\mathbf{M} = \text{from } \begin{array}{c} P \\ Q \\ R \end{array} \overset{\begin{array}{ccc} P & Q & R \end{array}}{\begin{bmatrix} 2 & 0 & 1 \\ 1 & 0 & 2 \\ 0 & 3 & 1 \end{bmatrix}} \quad \text{(to)}.$$

(a) Draw the network. (Draw single, un-arrowed, lines for two-way roads, and number the roads 1 to 7.)

(b) List the six two-stage routes from Q to itself.

(c) Evaluate $\mathbf{M}^2$, and explain why $\mathbf{M}^2$ is the two-stage route matrix.

Answers

Pre-test

1
$$\begin{bmatrix} 0 & 1 & 1 \\ 1 & 0 & 1 \\ 1 & 1 & 0 \end{bmatrix}$$

2 (a)
$$\begin{array}{c} \text{Anne} \\ \text{Zoe} \end{array} \overset{\begin{array}{ccc} \text{C}60 & \text{C}90 & \text{C}120 \end{array}}{\begin{bmatrix} 6 & 2 & 1 \\ 3 & 3 & 3 \end{bmatrix}}$$

(b) Anne bought seven C120s, and Zoe bought two C60s.

(c)
$$\begin{array}{c} \text{Anne} \\ \text{Zoe} \end{array} \overset{\begin{array}{ccc} \text{C}60 & \text{C}90 & \text{C}120 \end{array}}{\begin{bmatrix} 11 & 2 & 8 \\ 5 & 9 & 7 \end{bmatrix}}$$

3 Anne paid $6 \times 45\text{p} + 2 \times 70\text{p} + 1 \times 99\text{p} = £5.09$.
Zoe paid $3 \times (45\text{p} + 70\text{p} + 99\text{p}) = £6.42$.

4 (a)
$$\text{from } \begin{array}{c} G \\ H \\ J \end{array} \overset{\begin{array}{ccc} G & H & J \end{array}}{\begin{bmatrix} 0 & 1 & 0 \\ 1 & 2 & 2 \\ 0 & 2 & 0 \end{bmatrix}} \quad \text{(to)}$$

(b)
$$\text{from } \begin{array}{c} G \\ H \\ J \end{array} \overset{\begin{array}{ccc} G & H & J \end{array}}{\begin{bmatrix} 1 & 2 & 2 \\ 2 & 9 & 4 \\ 2 & 4 & 4 \end{bmatrix}} \quad \text{(to)}$$

5 (a) $17, 17, 13, {}^-13$ (b) $72, 72, 2, \frac{1}{2}$ (c) Commutative

6 (a) Yes   (b) No, $(36 \div 6) \div 2 = 3$, $36 \div (6 \div 2) = 12$ (c) Associative

2.1 Addition and subtraction

1 (a) $\begin{bmatrix} 2 & 3 & {}^-1 \\ 0 & {}^-4 & 5 \end{bmatrix}$ (b) $\begin{bmatrix} 0 & 0 & 0 \\ 0 & 0 & 0 \end{bmatrix}$ (c) $\begin{bmatrix} {}^-1 & 2 \\ 3 & {}^-4 \end{bmatrix}$

2 (a) $\mathbf{A} + \mathbf{B} = \begin{bmatrix} {}^-3 & 7 & 1 \\ {}^-\frac{1}{2} & 3 & {}^-2\frac{1}{2} \end{bmatrix}$, $(\mathbf{A} + \mathbf{B}) + \mathbf{C} = \begin{bmatrix} {}^-3 & 5 & 5 \\ {}^-3\frac{1}{2} & 12 & {}^-7\frac{1}{2} \end{bmatrix}$

(b) $\mathbf{B} + \mathbf{C} = \begin{bmatrix} {}^-7 & 4 & 5 \\ {}^-1\frac{1}{2} & 9 & {}^-8 \end{bmatrix}$, $\mathbf{A} + (\mathbf{B} + \mathbf{C}) = \begin{bmatrix} {}^-3 & 5 & 5 \\ {}^-3\frac{1}{2} & 12 & {}^-7\frac{1}{2} \end{bmatrix}$

3 (a) **B + A** is the same as **A + B**.
   (b) **C + B** is the same as **B + C**.

4 (a) $\begin{bmatrix} 5 & 2 & ^-2 \\ ^-2 & 0 & 4 \end{bmatrix}$ (b) $\begin{bmatrix} 3 & 2 & 1 \\ ^-1 & ^-2 & ^-3 \end{bmatrix}$ (c) $\begin{bmatrix} 2 & ^-1 \\ 0 & 3 \end{bmatrix}$ (d) $\begin{bmatrix} ^-2 & 1 \\ 0 & ^-3 \end{bmatrix}$

Exercise A

1 (a) **P + Q** = $\begin{bmatrix} 1 & 0 \\ ^-2 & ^-4 \\ 12 & 0 \end{bmatrix}$ (b) **P − Q** = $\begin{bmatrix} 1 & ^-4 \\ ^-4 & 4 \\ 2 & 2 \end{bmatrix}$ (c) **3P** = $\begin{bmatrix} 3 & ^-6 \\ ^-9 & 0 \\ 21 & 3 \end{bmatrix}$

2 They are not compatible because they are not of the same order, or shape. For example, the third row of **P** has nothing with which to combine in **R**.

3 (a) Inverse of **P** = $\begin{bmatrix} ^-1 & 2 \\ 3 & 0 \\ ^-7 & ^-1 \end{bmatrix}$ (b) Inverse of **R** = $\begin{bmatrix} ^-2 & 6 & ^-1 \\ 0 & ^-1 & 5 \end{bmatrix}$

4 $\begin{bmatrix} 0 & 0 & 0 & 0 & 0 \\ 0 & 0 & 0 & 0 & 0 \\ 0 & 0 & 0 & 0 & 0 \end{bmatrix}$ is the zero, or identity, matrix under addition for the set of 3×5 matrices.

5 (a) **Q + P** is the same as **P + Q** (see question 1(a)).
   (b) **Q − P** = $\begin{bmatrix} ^-1 & 4 \\ 4 & ^-4 \\ ^-2 & ^-2 \end{bmatrix}$

   This is not the same as **P − Q** because matrix subtraction is not commutative.

2.2 Multiplication

1 (a) For compatibility, the number of elements in the row of the first matrix must equal the number of elements in the column of the second matrix. Each element of the row must have a corresponding element of the column with which to combine, and neither row nor column must have any 'spare' elements. This is, in fact, the (only) rule for compatibility for all matrix multiplication.
   (b) For the combination to be meaningful, the headings of the columns of the first matrix must be the same as (and in the same order as) the headings of the rows of the second matrix.

   (c) **Z** = [3 3 3], **Q** = $\begin{bmatrix} 45 \\ 70 \\ 99 \end{bmatrix}$

   $\mathbf{R_z} = \mathbf{Z} \cdot \mathbf{Q} = [3 \quad 3 \quad 3] \begin{bmatrix} 45 \\ 70 \\ 99 \end{bmatrix} = [642]$,

   since $3 \times 45 + 3 \times 70 + 3 \times 99 = 642$.

2 (a) $[5 \ 0 \ 7] \begin{bmatrix} 60 \\ 89 \\ 115 \end{bmatrix} = [1105]$

So Anne spent £11.05 in 1980.

(b) $[2 \ 6 \ 4] \begin{bmatrix} 60 \\ 89 \\ 115 \end{bmatrix} = [1114]$

So Zoe spent £11.14 in 1980.

3

$\begin{matrix} \text{Anne} \\ \text{Zoe} \end{matrix} \begin{bmatrix} 5 & 0 & 7 \\ 2 & 6 & 4 \end{bmatrix} \begin{bmatrix} 60 \\ 89 \\ 115 \end{bmatrix} = \overset{\text{pence}}{\begin{bmatrix} 1105 \\ 1114 \end{bmatrix}}$

4 (a) $\mathbf{Q_2} = \begin{bmatrix} 52 \\ 79 \\ 105 \end{bmatrix}$ (b) $\mathbf{P} \cdot \mathbf{Q_2} = \begin{bmatrix} 6 & 2 & 1 \\ 3 & 3 & 3 \end{bmatrix} \begin{bmatrix} 52 \\ 79 \\ 105 \end{bmatrix}$

(c) $\mathbf{S} = \mathbf{P} \cdot \mathbf{Q_2} = \begin{bmatrix} 575 \\ 708 \end{bmatrix}$

5 (a) [Mary's row] . [1979 column] = $[y]$

Hence $[y] = [4 \ 28] \begin{bmatrix} 10 \\ 8 \end{bmatrix} = [4 \times 10 + 28 \times 8] = [264]$

(b)

	1973	1976	1979
Mr N	141	333	396
T = Mrs N	54	$122\frac{1}{2}$	148
Mary	98	216	264
Mark	85	$191\frac{1}{2}$	232

Exercise B

The order of the rows and columns may be different from that used in these answers, provided the same order is maintained through the question. In this answer we have listed the various members of the sets as they occur in the question.

1 (a)

$\begin{matrix} \mathbf{N} = \begin{matrix} \text{IA} \\ \text{G-A} \end{matrix} \end{matrix} \overset{\text{D} \quad \text{J} \quad \text{U}}{\begin{bmatrix} 4 & 2 & 7 \\ 1 & 3 & 6 \end{bmatrix}}$

(b)

$\mathbf{S} = \begin{matrix} \text{D} \\ \text{J} \\ \text{U} \end{matrix} \overset{\text{L} \quad \text{E}}{\begin{bmatrix} 9 & 24 \\ 12 & 12 \\ 0 & 32 \end{bmatrix}}$

(c) $\text{IA} [4 \ 2 \ 7] \overset{\text{E}}{\begin{bmatrix} 24 \\ 12 \\ 32 \end{bmatrix}} = [4 \times 24 + 2 \times 12 + 7 \times 32] = [344]$

So Inland Air can carry a maximum of 344 'economy' passengers.

(d) G-A $[1 \quad 3 \quad 6] \begin{bmatrix} \overset{L}{9} \\ 12 \\ 0 \end{bmatrix} = [1 \times 9 + 3 \times 12 + 6 \times 0] = [45]$

Go-Air can carry a maximum of 45 'luxury' passengers.

(e) $\mathbf{T} = \mathbf{N} \cdot \mathbf{S} = \begin{bmatrix} 4 & 2 & 7 \\ 1 & 3 & 6 \end{bmatrix} \begin{bmatrix} 9 & 24 \\ 12 & 12 \\ 0 & 32 \end{bmatrix} = \begin{array}{l} \\ \text{IA} \\ \text{G-A} \end{array} \begin{matrix} L & E \\ \begin{bmatrix} 60 & 344 \\ 45 & 252 \end{bmatrix} \end{matrix}$

(f) The matrix **T** states the maximum number of 'luxury' passengers, and the maximum number of 'economy' passengers, that each airline is able to carry.

➜ 2 (a) $\begin{bmatrix} 18 \\ 18 \end{bmatrix}$ (b) $[4 \quad {}^{-}8]$ (c) $\begin{bmatrix} {}^{-}4 & {}^{-}8 \\ 2 & 4 \end{bmatrix}$

2.3 Properties of matrix multiplication

❶ 1 (a) No (b) Yes, [11] (c) No (d) Yes, $\begin{bmatrix} 3 & 4 \\ 6 & 8 \end{bmatrix}$ (e) No

(f) Yes, $\begin{bmatrix} 3 & 4 & 5 \\ 6 & 8 & 10 \end{bmatrix}$

Parts (d) and (f) are a little surprising at first, but as in both cases the rows of the first matrix have only one element and the columns of the second matrix have only one element, multiplication is possible.

2 (a) Yes, 3×7 (b) No (c) No (d) Yes, 2×5 (e) Yes, 2×2 (f) Yes, 3×3

❷ 3 (a) As they both have 2 rows and 2 columns they have the same 'domino pattern' $(2 \times 2) \cdot (2 \times 2) \rightarrow (2 \times 2)$ and so both **A** . **B** and **B** . **A** are possible, giving a product of order (shape) 2×2 in both cases.

(b) $\mathbf{A} \cdot \mathbf{B} = \begin{bmatrix} {}^{-}7 & {}^{-}16 \\ 7 & 32 \end{bmatrix}$, $\mathbf{B} \cdot \mathbf{A} = \begin{bmatrix} {}^{-}1 & 2 \\ 43 & 26 \end{bmatrix}$

Although both products are possible, they are not equal.

❸ 4 (a) $(\mathbf{A} \cdot \mathbf{B}) \cdot \mathbf{C} = \begin{bmatrix} {}^{-}7 & {}^{-}16 \\ 7 & 32 \end{bmatrix} \begin{bmatrix} 2 & {}^{-}3 \\ 1 & 0 \end{bmatrix} = \begin{bmatrix} {}^{-}30 & 21 \\ 46 & {}^{-}21 \end{bmatrix}$,

$\mathbf{B} \cdot \mathbf{C} = \begin{bmatrix} {}^{-}2 & 3 \\ 14 & {}^{-}9 \end{bmatrix}$, $\mathbf{A} \cdot (\mathbf{B} \cdot \mathbf{C}) = \begin{bmatrix} 1 & {}^{-}2 \\ 5 & 4 \end{bmatrix} \begin{bmatrix} {}^{-}2 & 3 \\ 14 & {}^{-}9 \end{bmatrix} = \begin{bmatrix} {}^{-}30 & 21 \\ 46 & {}^{-}21 \end{bmatrix}$

(b) $\mathbf{C} \cdot (\mathbf{A} \cdot \mathbf{B}) = \begin{bmatrix} 2 & {}^{-}3 \\ 1 & 0 \end{bmatrix} \begin{bmatrix} {}^{-}7 & {}^{-}16 \\ 7 & 32 \end{bmatrix} = \begin{bmatrix} {}^{-}35 & {}^{-}128 \\ {}^{-}7 & {}^{-}16 \end{bmatrix}$,

$(\mathbf{B} \cdot \mathbf{C}) \cdot \mathbf{A} = \begin{bmatrix} {}^{-}2 & 3 \\ 14 & {}^{-}9 \end{bmatrix} \begin{bmatrix} 1 & {}^{-}2 \\ 5 & 4 \end{bmatrix} = \begin{bmatrix} 13 & 16 \\ {}^{-}31 & {}^{-}64 \end{bmatrix}$

$(\mathbf{A} \cdot \mathbf{B}) \cdot \mathbf{C} = \mathbf{A} \cdot (\mathbf{B} \cdot \mathbf{C})$, but changing the order of **A**, **B** and **C** produces a different result.

Exercise C

1 Products (a), (d), (e) and (f) are possible.
 (a) $(2 \times 2) \cdot (2 \times 3) \to (2 \times 3)$
 (b) $(2 \times 2) \cdot (3 \times 2)$ – these matrices are not compatible.
 (c) $(2 \times 3) \cdot (2 \times 2)$ – these matrices are not compatible.
 (d) $(2 \times 3) \cdot (3 \times 2) \to (2 \times 2)$
 (e) $(3 \times 2) \cdot (2 \times 2) \to (3 \times 2)$
 (f) $(3 \times 2) \cdot (2 \times 3) \to (3 \times 3)$

2 Parts (d) and (f) of question 1 show that the product $\mathbf{Q} \cdot \mathbf{R}$ is a 2×2 matrix, whereas
 $\mathbf{R} \cdot \mathbf{Q}$ is a 3×3 matrix. Obviously $\mathbf{Q} \cdot \mathbf{R} \neq \mathbf{R} \cdot \mathbf{Q}$, so matrix multiplication is not
 commutative.

3 (a) $\mathbf{P} \cdot \mathbf{Q} = \begin{bmatrix} 1 & ^-1 & 1 \\ 8 & ^-5 & 2 \end{bmatrix}$
 (d) $\mathbf{Q} \cdot \mathbf{R} = \begin{bmatrix} 2 & 1 \\ ^-6 & 5 \end{bmatrix}$

 (e) $\mathbf{R} \cdot \mathbf{P} = \begin{bmatrix} ^-1 & 6 \\ 2 & ^-3 \\ 7 & ^-12 \end{bmatrix}$
 (f) $\mathbf{R} \cdot \mathbf{Q} = \begin{bmatrix} 7 & ^-5 & 3 \\ ^-2 & 1 & 0 \\ ^-9 & 5 & ^-1 \end{bmatrix}$

2.4 Identity and inverse of 2 × 2 matrices

1
$$\begin{array}{ccccccc} \text{(a)} & \text{(b)} & \text{(c)} & \text{(d)} & \text{(e)} & \text{(f)} & \text{(g)} \end{array}$$
$$\mathbf{X} \cdot \mathbf{Y} = \begin{bmatrix} 3 & 3 \\ ^-1 & ^-1 \end{bmatrix} \begin{bmatrix} 5 & 5 \\ ^-4 & ^-4 \end{bmatrix} \begin{bmatrix} 5 & ^-2 \\ ^-4 & 3 \end{bmatrix} \begin{bmatrix} ^-2 & 5 \\ 3 & ^-4 \end{bmatrix} \begin{bmatrix} 0 & 3 \\ 0 & ^-1 \end{bmatrix} \begin{bmatrix} 5 & 0 \\ ^-4 & 0 \end{bmatrix} \begin{bmatrix} ^-2 & 3 \\ 3 & ^-1 \end{bmatrix}$$

$$\begin{array}{ccccccc} \text{(a)} & \text{(b)} & \text{(c)} & \text{(d)} & \text{(e)} & \text{(f)} & \text{(g)} \end{array}$$
$$\mathbf{Y} \cdot \mathbf{X} = \begin{bmatrix} 1 & 1 \\ 1 & 1 \end{bmatrix} \begin{bmatrix} 1 & 1 \\ 0 & 0 \end{bmatrix} \begin{bmatrix} 5 & ^-2 \\ ^-4 & 3 \end{bmatrix} \begin{bmatrix} ^-4 & 3 \\ 5 & ^-2 \end{bmatrix} \begin{bmatrix} ^-4 & 3 \\ ^-4 & 3 \end{bmatrix} \begin{bmatrix} 5 & ^-2 \\ 0 & 0 \end{bmatrix} \begin{bmatrix} ^-4 & 3 \\ 1 & 1 \end{bmatrix}$$

2 (a) $\mathbf{X} \cdot \mathbf{Y} = \begin{bmatrix} 9 & 5 \\ 25 & 14 \end{bmatrix} = \mathbf{Y} \cdot \mathbf{X}$ (b) $\mathbf{X} \cdot \mathbf{Y} = \begin{bmatrix} 1 & 0 \\ 0 & 1 \end{bmatrix} = \mathbf{Y} \cdot \mathbf{X}$

3 (a) $\begin{bmatrix} 2 & 0 \\ 0 & 2 \end{bmatrix}$ (b) $\begin{bmatrix} 4 & 0 \\ 0 & 4 \end{bmatrix}$ (c) $\begin{bmatrix} 1 & 0 \\ 0 & 1 \end{bmatrix}$

4 (a) $\begin{bmatrix} 4 & 0 \\ 0 & 4 \end{bmatrix}$ (b) $\begin{bmatrix} 14 & 0 \\ 0 & 14 \end{bmatrix}$ (c) $\begin{bmatrix} ^-2 & 0 \\ 0 & ^-2 \end{bmatrix}$

5 (a) $\Delta = (8 \times 2) - (^-3 \times ^-4) = 16 - 12 = 4$.
  The inverse is $\frac{1}{4} \begin{bmatrix} 2 & 3 \\ 4 & 8 \end{bmatrix}$ or $\begin{bmatrix} \frac{1}{2} & \frac{3}{4} \\ 1 & 2 \end{bmatrix}$.

 (b) $\Delta = 14$. The inverse is $\frac{1}{14} \begin{bmatrix} 1 & 3 \\ ^-4 & 2 \end{bmatrix}$.

 (c) $\Delta = ^-2$. The inverse is $\frac{1}{^-2} \begin{bmatrix} 4 & ^-2 \\ ^-3 & 1 \end{bmatrix}$ or $\begin{bmatrix} ^-2 & 1 \\ 1\frac{1}{2} & ^-\frac{1}{2} \end{bmatrix}$.

 (d) $\Delta = 0$. There is no inverse.

Exercise D

1 (a) $\Delta = 1$. The inverse is $\begin{bmatrix} 3 & ^-1 \\ ^-5 & 2 \end{bmatrix}$.

(b) $\Delta = 1$. The inverse is $\begin{bmatrix} 3 & 5 \\ 4 & 7 \end{bmatrix}$.

(c) $\Delta = (5 \times 0) - (2 \times {}^-1) = 0 - ({}^-2) = 2$.

The inverse is $\frac{1}{2}\begin{bmatrix} 0 & ^-2 \\ 1 & 5 \end{bmatrix} = \begin{bmatrix} 0 & ^-1 \\ \frac{1}{2} & 2\frac{1}{2} \end{bmatrix}$.

(d) $\Delta = ({}^-24) - ({}^-24) = 0$. There is no inverse.

(e) $\Delta = {}^-4$. The inverse is $\frac{1}{{}^-4}\begin{bmatrix} 8 & ^-12 \\ ^-3 & 4 \end{bmatrix} = \begin{bmatrix} ^-2 & 3 \\ \frac{3}{4} & ^-1 \end{bmatrix}$.

(f) $\Delta = {}^-1$. The inverse is $\frac{1}{{}^-1}\begin{bmatrix} ^-3 & ^-5 \\ ^-2 & ^-3 \end{bmatrix} = \begin{bmatrix} 3 & 5 \\ 2 & 3 \end{bmatrix}$.

(g) $\Delta = ({}^-33) - ({}^-35) = 2$. The inverse is $\begin{bmatrix} 5\frac{1}{2} & 2\frac{1}{2} \\ ^-3\frac{1}{2} & ^-1\frac{1}{2} \end{bmatrix}$.

(h) $\Delta = 5$. The inverse is $\frac{1}{5}\begin{bmatrix} 1 & 2 \\ ^-1 & 3 \end{bmatrix}$.

The last inverse could be put in the decimal form $\begin{bmatrix} 0.2 & 0.4 \\ ^-0.2 & 0.6 \end{bmatrix}$ as the decimals

are exact, and simple. Generally, though, it is better to leave the elements of the inverse as fractions or mixed numbers, unless specifically instructed otherwise.

2 $I_3 = \begin{bmatrix} 1 & 0 & 0 \\ 0 & 1 & 0 \\ 0 & 0 & 1 \end{bmatrix}$, $I_3 \cdot Q = Q$ and $Q \cdot I_3 = Q$

3 (a) $A \cdot B = \begin{bmatrix} 4 & 0 & 0 \\ 0 & 4 & 0 \\ 0 & 0 & 4 \end{bmatrix}$

(b) The inverse of A is A^{-1} such that $A \cdot A^{-1} = I_3$.

Since $A \cdot B = 4I_3$, it follows that

$$A^{-1} = \tfrac{1}{4}B = \begin{bmatrix} \frac{1}{2} & 1 & 0 \\ ^-\frac{1}{4} & \frac{1}{4} & ^-\frac{1}{4} \\ 0 & 1 & 0 \end{bmatrix}.$$

(c) Similarly $B^{-1} = \tfrac{1}{4}A = \begin{bmatrix} \frac{1}{2} & 0 & ^-\frac{1}{2} \\ 0 & 0 & \frac{1}{4} \\ ^-\frac{1}{2} & ^-1 & \frac{3}{4} \end{bmatrix}.$

Post-test

1 $D + E = E + D = \begin{bmatrix} 5 & 8 \\ ^-2 & ^-3\frac{1}{2} \end{bmatrix}$, $D - E = \begin{bmatrix} ^-3 & 2 \\ 2 & ^-\frac{1}{2} \end{bmatrix}$, $E - D = \begin{bmatrix} 3 & ^-2 \\ ^-2 & \frac{1}{2} \end{bmatrix}$,

$D \cdot E = \begin{bmatrix} ^-6 & ^-4\frac{1}{2} \\ 4 & 3 \end{bmatrix}$, $E \cdot D = \begin{bmatrix} 4 & 14 \\ ^-2 & ^-7 \end{bmatrix}$

2 (a) $\mathbf{D}^2 = \begin{bmatrix} 1 & ^-5 \\ 0 & 4 \end{bmatrix}$ (b) $4\mathbf{E} = \begin{bmatrix} 16 & 12 \\ ^-8 & ^-6 \end{bmatrix}$

  (c) $\mathbf{E} \cdot \mathbf{F}$ is compatible $[(2 \times 2) \cdot (2 \times 3) \rightarrow (2 \times 3)]$.

$$\mathbf{E} \cdot \mathbf{F} = \begin{bmatrix} 1 & 12 & 10 \\ -\frac{1}{2} & ^-6 & ^-5 \end{bmatrix}$$

  (d) As $\mathbf{F}$ is of order 2×3 the 'domino pattern' for $\mathbf{F} \cdot \mathbf{F}$ is $(2 \times 3) \cdot (2 \times 3)$ which is incompatible for multiplication.

3 (a) $\begin{bmatrix} 0 & 0 & 0 \\ 0 & 0 & 0 \end{bmatrix}$ (b) Under addition, the inverse of $\mathbf{F}$ is $\begin{bmatrix} 2 & 0 & ^-1 \\ ^-3 & ^-4 & ^-2 \end{bmatrix}$.

4 (a) For $\mathbf{D}$, $\Delta = (1 \times ^-2) - (5 \times 0) = ^-2$.

     For $\mathbf{E}$, $\Delta = (4 \times ^-1\frac{1}{2}) - (3 \times ^-2) = 0$.

  (b) Hence $\mathbf{E}$ is a singular matrix.

  (c) The inverse of $\mathbf{D}$ is $\dfrac{1}{^-2} \begin{bmatrix} ^-2 & ^-5 \\ 0 & 1 \end{bmatrix} = \begin{bmatrix} 1 & 2\frac{1}{2} \\ 0 & ^-\frac{1}{2} \end{bmatrix}$.

3 Reflection

Objectives

This is what you should be able to do after studying this chapter.
(1) Understand what is meant by transformation geometry.
(2) Know that reflection is one type of transformation.
(3) Find the image of a point when reflected in a given mirror line, and hence reflect a shape in a given mirror line.
(4) Deduce the coordinates of the image of (x, y) under reflection in simple cases.
(5) Find, when possible, the mirror line that reflects a given point or shape into a given image.
(6) Apply matrix ideas to reflection geometry, and know the matrices that represent reflections in some of the lines through the origin.
(7) Know the properties of reflection concerning shape, size and sense of the image; and know that reflection is a self-inverse operation.

Pre-test

> 1   Make freehand sketches of the shapes in Figure 1, and, where possible, draw in the line or lines of symmetry.

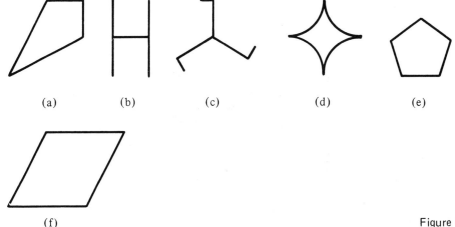

(a)   (b)   (c)   (d)   (e)

(f)   Figure 1

2 (a) Copy Figure 2 and use a set square to draw a line through P at right angles (perpendicular) to m.
  (b) Where does this line meet the x axis?

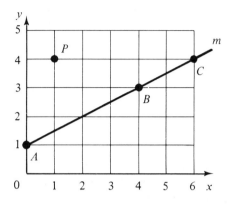

Figure 2

3 From Figure 2 write down the following.
  (a) The coordinates of A, B and C.
  (b) The equation of the line m.
  (c) The coordinates of a point Q which is such that QB is at right angles to the line m and $QB = BC$ in length. (You should be able to find two answers.)
  (d) The position vectors of B and C, and the displacement vector for $\mathbf{BC}$.

4 The function f is such that $f: (x, y) \rightarrow (6 - x, y)$. Find the following.
  (a) $f(0, 4)$ (b) $f(1, 3)$ (c) $f(3, 2)$ (d) $f(7, 1)$
  (e) Plot these ordered pairs and their images as points on an xy graph. What is the inverse of f?

5 Evaluate these. (a) $\begin{bmatrix} 3 & 2 \\ 0 & 1 \end{bmatrix}\begin{bmatrix} -4 \\ 5 \end{bmatrix}$ (b) $\begin{bmatrix} 3 & 2 \\ 0 & 1 \end{bmatrix}\begin{bmatrix} x \\ y \end{bmatrix}$

3.1 Transformation geometry

The letter F in the bottom left-hand corner of Figure 3 can be moved, mapped, or *transformed*, onto each of the other letters by some method or other.

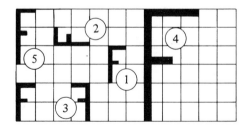

Figure 3

Thus F can be pushed, slid, or *translated*, onto F_1. It can be turned, or *rotated*, onto F_2. It can be turned over, or *reflected*, onto F_3. It can be magnified, or *enlarged*, onto F_4, and it can be *stretched* onto F_5, and so on.

Each of these movements, or methods, is a different transformation, which operates under its own set of rules. Geometry is the study of shapes, and so transformation geometry is a study of what happens to shapes under various transformations. In this chapter we shall be considering one of these transformations, that of reflection. Rotation will be studied in the remainder of this book, and other transformations will be looked at in *Further Matrices and Transformations*.

3.2 Reflection and symmetry

Figure 4 has one line of symmetry.

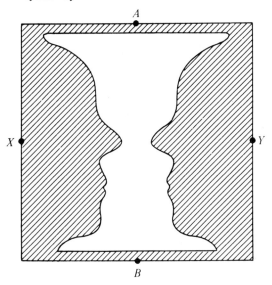

Figure 4

> 1 Stand a mirror on *AB* and then on *XY*. Which of these is the line of symmetry?

2 In Figure 5, stand your mirror on the lines with arrows at the ends. Which of these are lines of symmetry?

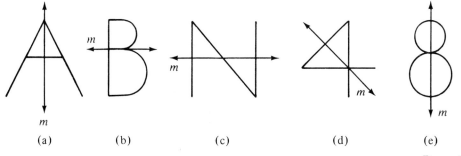

(a)　　　　(b)　　　　(c)　　　　(d)　　　　(e)

Figure 5

From these results we see that if a mirror is placed on a line of symmetry then one half of the figure is reflected exactly on top of the other half.

45

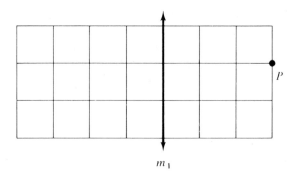

m_1

Figure 6

 3   Copy Figure 6.
  (a) Stand your mirror on the line m_1. Look at the reflection of P in the mirror, and put a dot on the paper where you think this reflection is. Label this point P_1. As reflection is an operation that maps P onto P_1, we can call P the object and P_1 the image under reflection.
  (b) On your diagram draw and label some other lines $m_2, m_3, \ldots$, parallel to m_1. Stand your mirror on these lines and label dots P_2, P_3, $\ldots$ to show the images of P when the mirror is on the lines $m_2, m_3, \ldots$ Is the image of P always the same distance from the mirror as P?

4   (a) If you stand in front of a large mirror and move towards it, what does your image do?
  (b) If your nose is 60 cm in front of the mirror, where does its image appear to be?
  (c) Imagine a line joining your nose to its reflection. What angle does this line make with the mirror?

 5   (a) Copy Figure 7 and mark in the images of P, Q and R under reflection in the mirror line m.
  (b) Join up P, Q and R to form a triangle T. What is the image of T?

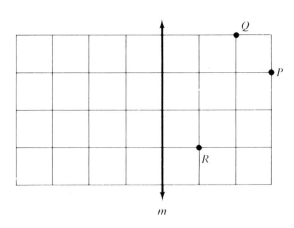

m

Figure 7

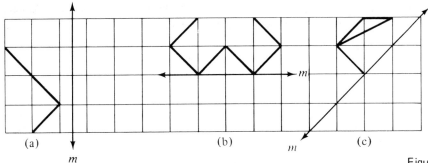

(a)　　　　　　　(b)　　　　　　(c)

m

Figure 8

6   Copy Figure 8 and draw in the images of the shapes in the mirror lines marked.

To summarise, in a reflection the point P maps onto the point P' so that the line PP' is at right angles to the mirror. The distance PN is the same as the distance $P'N$. (See Figure 9.)

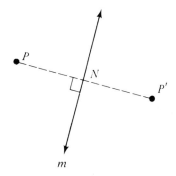

m

Figure 9

Mathematical reflections

In most cases, reflection in a real mirror works from one side only. If you stand behind the mirror you will see nothing. However, our mathematical mirrors are always double-sided, so that they reflect both ways. In other words, not only does P reflect onto P', but Q also reflects onto Q' (see Figure 10). Another oddity of mathematical mirrors is that they are assumed to have no thickness.

7   In Figure 10, where is the image of (a) P',   (b) Q'?

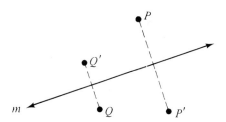

Figure 10

8   Copy Figure 11 (tracing paper will be helpful). Draw in the reflections, assuming that
     the arrowed lines represent double-sided mirrors.

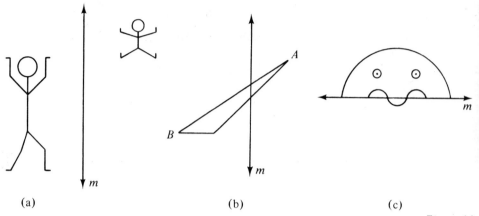

(a)   (b)   (c)

Figure 11

From now on, mirror lines will be denoted by unlabelled lines with arrows at both
ends.

Exercise A

▷ 1   Stand your mirror on the arrowed lines in Figure 12. Which of these are lines of
     symmetry?

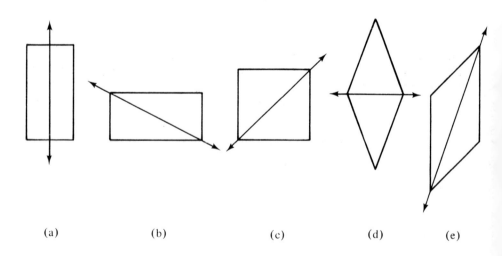

(a)   (b)   (c)   (d)   (e)

Figure 12

2 Copy Figure 13 freehand, and draw in the images for the mirror lines marked.

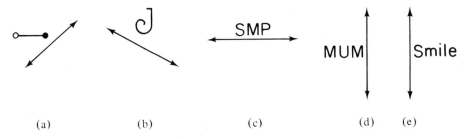

(a)   (b)   (c)   (d)   (e)

Figure 13

3 Mark two points A and B on a piece of tracing paper. Fold the paper to find a mirror line so that B is the image of A. How many possible positions are there for the mirror line?

4 In Figure 14, $A'B'$ is the reflection of AB in the mirror.

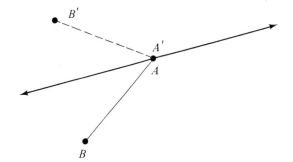

Figure 14

(a) If the angle between AB and the mirror is $35°$, what is the angle between $A'B'$ and the mirror?
(b) If the mirror is rotated about A until BAB' is a straight line, what is the angle between the mirror and AB?
(c) Through what angle was the mirror turned?
(d) Through what angle has $A'B'$ turned?

5 Copy Figure 15 and draw in the reflections.

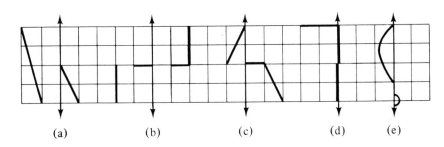

(a)   (b)   (c)   (d)   (e)

Figure 15

6 (a) In Figure 16(a) the line makes an angle of 24° with the mirror. What angle does its image make with the mirror?

(b) The angle between a line in an object and the corresponding line in the image is 72°. Describe carefully the position of the mirror line. (See Figure 16(b).)

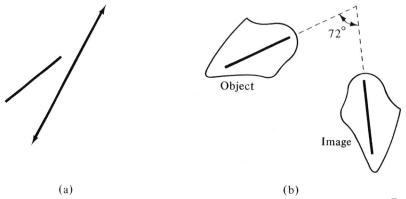

(a)   (b)

Figure 16

7   A fly walks around the circle in Figure 17 in a clockwise direction. Copy the diagram and draw the path of the image of the fly, indicating the direction in which the image walks. Which gets round the circle first, the fly or its image?

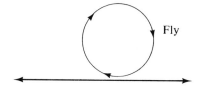

Figure 17

3.3 Reflections using coordinates

 1 (a) Stand a mirror on the line $x = 0$ in Figure 18, and note where the images of A, B, C, D and E are.

(b) Make a copy of Figure 18, and mark in A, B, C, D and E and their images. Write down the coordinates of the images.

(c) Join each point to its image by a line. What is the relation of the mirror to each of these lines?

(d) If the point Z has coordinates (x, y), what are the coordinates of its image under this reflection?

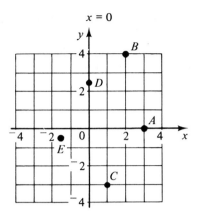

$x = 0$

Figure 18

> 2 (a) If a mirror is standing on the line $y = x$ (see Figure 19), where would the reflections of P, Q, R and S appear to be?
>   (b) Write down the coordinates of the four points and their images.
>   (c) What are the coordinates of the image of $Z(x, y)$ under this reflection?

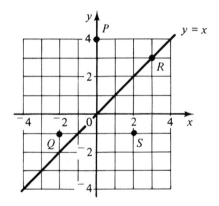

Figure 19

3 (a) Draw x and y axes for values of x from $^-2$ to 8 and y from $^-4$ to 4. On your diagram, draw the triangle whose corners are $A(^-1, ^-1), B(4, 4), C(3, ^-3)$.
   (b) Draw the reflection of the triangle ABC when the mirror is the line $x = 3$.
   (c) Where do the lines AB and $A'B'$ meet?
   (d) Show that the image of $Z(3 + k, y)$ is $Z'(3 - k, y)$.

From these results we see that in some special cases we can find a 'formula' for the coordinates of the image of a point. For example, we can summarise the results of questions 1, 2 and 3 as follows.

Mirror line	$x = 0$ (the y axis)	$y = x$	$x = 3$
Image of (x, y)	$(^-x, y)$	(y, x)	
Image of $(3 + k, y)$			$(3 - k, y)$

This last result is not very useful as it stands, but if we put x for $3 + k$, we can see that $k = x - 3$, and so, under reflection in $x = 3$, the image of (x, y) is $(6 - x, y)$. Compare

51

question **4** of the pre-test, and note that this result is true for points (x, y) on both sides of the mirror.

The results for reflection in the x axis ($y = 0$) and the diagonal $y = {}^-x$ (or $x + y = 0$) are deduced in questions **1** and **2** of Exercise B.

Exercise B

1 (a) Draw x and y axes for $^-5$ to 5 on both axes. Plot the points $C(4, 3)$, $D(^-4, 0)$,
       $E(0, {}^-1)$, $F(2, {}^-4)$, $G(5, {}^-5)$ and $H(5, 1)$. Join these up to form the hexagon
       CDEFGH and draw its reflection in the mirror line $y = 0$ (the x axis).
    (b) What is the image of $Z(x, y)$ under this reflection?

2 Repeat question **1** for the mirror line $y = {}^-x$ (i.e. $x + y = 0$).

3.4 Matrix representation

In the last section we noticed that, whatever the values of x and y, the reflection in the line $x = 0$ (the y axis) of the point $Z(x, y)$ is the point with coordinates $(^-x, y)$.

We can express this in several ways. Firstly, if the image of Z is Z', with coordinates (x', y'), then

$$(x', y') = (^-x, y).$$

Alternatively, if M_y denotes reflection in the y axis, then

$$M_y: (x, y) \rightarrow (^-x, y),$$

$$\text{i.e. } M_y \ (x, y) = (^-x, y).$$

This is beginning to look like something to do with matrices. At the moment, however, one difficulty is that (x, y) is not a vector but a pair of coordinates (that comma is important!) and even if it were, the domino rule would require M_y to be a 1×1 matrix – and it is impossible to find a single number (k say) such that $[k] \cdot [x \ y] = [^-x \ y]$, as k cannot be $^+1$ and $^-1$ at the same time.

But another way of writing $(x', y') = (^-x, y)$ is

$$\begin{cases} x' = {}^-x \\ y' = y \end{cases} \qquad \text{or} \qquad \begin{bmatrix} x' \\ y' \end{bmatrix} = \begin{bmatrix} {}^-x \\ y \end{bmatrix}.$$

We are now writing down a statement about the position vector of Z'. Can we now find a matrix M_y such that $\quad M_y \begin{bmatrix} x \\ y \end{bmatrix} = \begin{bmatrix} {}^-x \\ y \end{bmatrix}$?

This time, by the domino rule, we require a 2×2 matrix, and it is not difficult to see that the following works:

$$\begin{bmatrix} {}^-1 & 0 \\ 0 & 1 \end{bmatrix} \begin{bmatrix} x \\ y \end{bmatrix} = \begin{bmatrix} {}^-x \\ y \end{bmatrix}.$$

Hence we say that the matrix for (or the matrix that represents) reflection in the line $x = 0$ is

$$\begin{bmatrix} {}^-1 & 0 \\ 0 & 1 \end{bmatrix}.$$

This is a new view of a matrix. We cannot give labels (or headings) to the rows and columns and so it cannot really be described as an information matrix. It is more like an operator or a function as it needs something to operate on, in the same way that the square root symbol $\sqrt{}$ needs something to work on. Thus $\sqrt{x}$ is an instruction to find the square root of x, and $\mathbf{M}_y$ (Z) is an instruction to find the image of Z under the transformation whose matrix is $\mathbf{M}_y$. Such matrices are sometimes called *instruction matrices*. The interesting and important point, however, is that these matrices behave in exactly the same manner as information matrices, and so all the results of Chapter 2 are also applicable to instruction matrices.

Using the matrix

First let us check the coordinates of the images in the example at the beginning of Section 3.3.

A' is the image of $A(3, 0)$ under the mapping $\mathbf{M}_y$, i.e. $A' = \mathbf{M}_y(A)$. So the position vector of A' is given by

$$\begin{bmatrix} ^-1 & 0 \\ 0 & 1 \end{bmatrix} \begin{bmatrix} 3 \\ 0 \end{bmatrix} = \begin{bmatrix} ^-3 \\ 0 \end{bmatrix},$$

and the coordinates of A' are therefore $(^-3, 0)$. Does this agree with your previous result?

The coordinates of the other four images, B', C', D' and E', could be worked out similarly by four more little sums like this. However, as one of the points of matrix algebra is shorthand, all the work can be written down as one piece:

$$\begin{bmatrix} ^-1 & 0 \\ 0 & 1 \end{bmatrix} \begin{matrix} A & B & C & D & E \\ \begin{bmatrix} 3 & 2 & 1 & 0 & ^-1\frac{1}{2} \\ 0 & 4 & ^-3 & 2\frac{1}{2} & ^-\frac{1}{2} \end{bmatrix} \end{matrix} = \begin{matrix} A' & B' & C' & D' & E' \\ \begin{bmatrix} ^-3 & & & & \\ 0 & & & & \end{bmatrix} \end{matrix}$$

Note that a matrix used in this manner operates on the *position vectors* of the points, and the 'answers' are given as position vectors, all of which are *column* vectors.

> 1 Copy and complete the matrix above to find the coordinates of B', C', D' and E'. Check these with your earlier results.

2 (a) From question 2 of Section 3.3 write down the image of $Z(x, y)$ under reflection in the line $y = x$.
   (b) Hence derive the matrix for this reflection.
   (c) Check the coordinates of P', Q', R' and S'.

3 Evaluate these.
   (a) $\begin{bmatrix} ^-1 & 0 \\ 0 & 1 \end{bmatrix} \begin{bmatrix} 0 \\ 0 \end{bmatrix}$ (b) $\begin{bmatrix} 0 & 1 \\ 1 & 0 \end{bmatrix} \begin{bmatrix} 0 \\ 0 \end{bmatrix}$ (c) $\begin{bmatrix} a & b \\ c & d \end{bmatrix} \begin{bmatrix} 0 \\ 0 \end{bmatrix}$

Question 3 shows that the origin (the point with coordinates $(0, 0)$) is invariant (not moved or transformed anywhere) when operated on by any 2×2 matrix. Hence one condition for it to be possible to represent a transformation by a 2×2 matrix is that the origin must be invariant under the transformation. These general ideas will be considered more fully in *Further Matrices and Transformations* – at the moment we shall just state that not all transformations can be represented by 2×2 matrices, and not all 2×2

matrices represent recognisable transformations. So far as reflections are concerned, if the mirror line passes through the origin, then – and only then – is it possible to represent the reflection by a 2 × 2 matrix.

Exercise C

▷ 1   Use your results from Exercise B to find the matrices for reflection in (a) the *x* axis ($y = 0$), (b) the line $x + y = 0$.
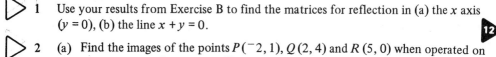

▷ 2   (a) Find the images of the points $P(^-2, 1)$, $Q(2, 4)$ and $R(5, 0)$ when operated on
       by the matrix $\begin{bmatrix} ^-0.6 & 0.8 \\ 0.8 & 0.6 \end{bmatrix}$.

       (b) Draw a diagram to show the triangle *PQR* and its image, and hence identify the
       transformation represented by this matrix.

3.5 Properties of reflection

In studying various transformations one of the things we look for is *invariance* – in other words what properties are unaltered under a transformation.

For example under an enlargement (see Figure 3 where F_4 is an enlargement of F) the size of a figure is changed, but the shape remains the same, whereas under a stretch (F_5 in Figure 3) both size and shape are changed.

▷ 1   Which of the following are invariant under reflection – lengths, angles, areas, position, shape, size?

Is 'sense' invariant under reflection? By this we mean: if the object is lettered clockwise, is the corresponding lettering of the image clockwise or anti-clockwise?

▷ 2   Look at your answer to question 2 of Exercise C. Is 'sense' invariant under reflection?

3   Is 'parallelism' invariant? In other words, if a line *AB* is parallel to a line *XY* in the object, is it always true that $A'B'$ is parallel to $X'Y'$ under reflection?

When size and shape are invariant, an object and its image are said to be *congruent*. This means that if the object is cut out, it will fit exactly on top of its image. If this can be done without turning the object over, the sense is preserved (invariant) and the shapes are said to be *directly congruent*. Otherwise, as in reflection, they are *oppositely congruent*.

A transformation, such as reflection, under which the object and image are congruent is sometimes called an *isometry*.

Summary

(1) Transformation geometry is a method of mapping every point of a plane (or a space), and hence shapes, to another position. Each transformation has its own set of rules, or conditions. The original point/shape is called the object, and the final position is called the image.

(2) Reflection is one type of transformation. To define a particular reflection we need to know the mirror line, or line of symmetry, m.

(3) If P' is the reflection of P in m, then the rule for finding P' is that it is directly opposite to P in the mirror, and equidistant from the mirror (see Figure 20). That is, the mirror is the perpendicular bisector (mediator) of the line joining P to P'. In mathematical reflections, the mirrors are two-sided.

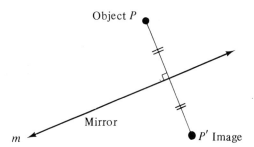

Object P

Mirror

m P' Image

Figure 20

(4) A reflection in a line through the origin may be represented by a 2×2 matrix **M**. If **X** gives the position vector(s) of an object, then the position vector(s) of the image are given by **M** · **X**.

(5) The images of the point (x, y) and the matrix for the reflection for some particular cases are:

Mirror line	x axis $(y = 0)$	y axis	$y = x$	$x + y = 0$
Image of (x, y)	$(x, \,^-y)$	$(^-x, y)$	(y, x)	$(^-y, \,^-x)$
Matrix	$\begin{bmatrix} 1 & 0 \\ 0 & ^-1 \end{bmatrix}$	$\begin{bmatrix} ^-1 & 0 \\ 0 & 1 \end{bmatrix}$	$\begin{bmatrix} 0 & 1 \\ 1 & 0 \end{bmatrix}$	$\begin{bmatrix} 0 & ^-1 \\ ^-1 & 0 \end{bmatrix}$

(6) If P_1 is the reflection of P then the mirror line will be the mediator of PP_1. Hence P_1Q_1...will be the reflection of PQ...only if the mediators of PP_1, QQ_1,...are all the same line. If this is so, then the mediator is the mirror line. (If the two shapes are congruent, it is sufficient for any two of the mediators to be coincident.)

(7) Under reflection, size and shape (and hence lengths, angles and areas) are unaltered, but sense is reversed. All points on the mirror line are invariant. All lines at right angles to the mirror line are invariant as a whole (although individual points on the lines are not).

(8) Reflection is a self-inverse operation.

Post-test

1 Make freehand sketches of the shapes in Figure 21, and construct their images, using tracing paper, or ruler and set square.

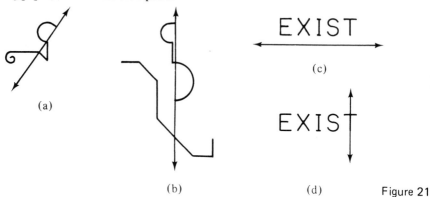

(a)

(b)

(c)

(d)

Figure 21

2 (a) Copy Figure 22 and construct the reflection of the letter F in the mirror line $y = x$.
   (b) Verify your answer by using the matrix
   $$\begin{bmatrix} 0 & 1 \\ 1 & 0 \end{bmatrix}.$$

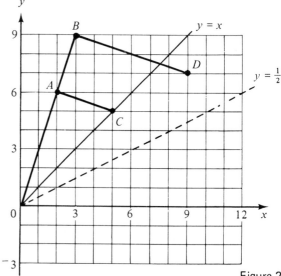

Figure 22

3 Repeat question 2 for the mirror line $y = \frac{1}{2}x$ and the matrix $\begin{bmatrix} 0.6 & 0.8 \\ 0.8 & ^-0.6 \end{bmatrix}$.

4 In Figure 23 state, where possible, the mirror line when the reflection of F is (a) F_1, (b) F_2, (c) F_3, (d) F_4.

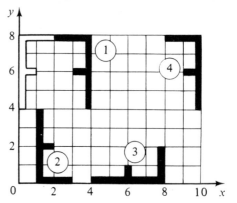

Figure 23

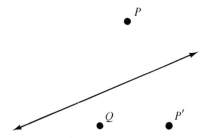

Figure 24

5 In Figure 24, given that P' is the reflection of P in the mirror line, find the reflection of Q using a straight edge only (that is, without using a graduated ruler, or set square, or protractor, etc.). **16**

Assignment

1 Copy and complete Figure 25, adding the reflections of the shapes in the mirror lines shown.

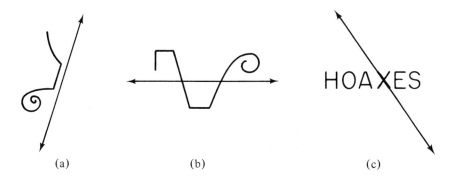

(a)　　　　　　　(b)　　　　　　　(c)

Figure 25

2 Find the mirror lines in Figure 26 so that each pair of shapes is an object and its reflection.

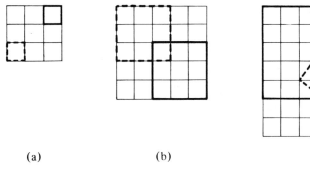 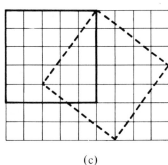

(a)　　　　　　　(b)　　　　　　　(c)

Figure 26

3   Copy and complete the following table.

Object	(5, ⁻1)	(⁻4, 3)		(8, ⁻3)	(5 : 5)	
Mirror line		y = x	y = 2		x = 4	x + y =
Image	(5, 1)		(9, 2)	(3, ⁻8)		(1, ⁻2

4   (a) Draw x and y axes for values of x from ⁻4 to 10, and for values of y from ⁻4 to 8.
Mark the points F (3, ⁻4), G (7½, 2½) and H (8, 6).

(b) Construct on your diagram the reflection of the triangle FGH in the mirror line $y = \frac{3}{4}x$.

(c) Find the image of FGH when operated on by the matrix

$$\begin{bmatrix} 0.8 & 0.6 \\ 0.6 & ⁻0.8 \end{bmatrix}.$$

(d) Mark this image on your diagram, and hence deduce the transformation represented by this matrix.

Answers

Pre-test

1   The lines of symmetry for (a), (b), (d) and (e) are shown by the dotted lines in Figure A. Figures (c) and (f) have no lines of symmetry.

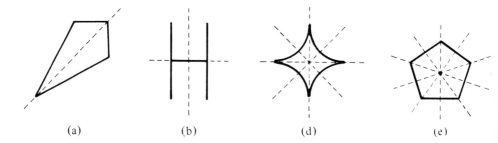

(a)   (b)   (d)   (e)

Figure A

2   (a) Place the set square as shown in Figure B.
(b) The line should meet the x axis at the point (3, 0).

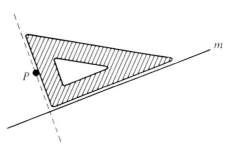

Figure B

58

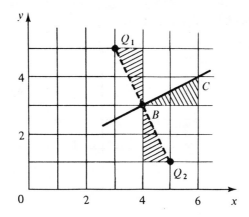

Figure C

3   (a) A is $(0, 1)$, B is $(4, 3)$ and C is $(6, 4)$.

    (b) The line m is $y = \frac{1}{2}x + 1$. (Some alternative forms of this equation are $2y = x + 2$, $2y - x = 2$, $x - 2y = {}^{-}2$).

    (c) Q could be $(3, 5)$ or $(5, 1)$. See Figure C above.

    (d) $\mathbf{OB} = \begin{bmatrix} 4 \\ 3 \end{bmatrix}$, $\mathbf{OC} = \begin{bmatrix} 6 \\ 4 \end{bmatrix}$, $\mathbf{BC} = \begin{bmatrix} 2 \\ 1 \end{bmatrix}$.

4   (a) $f(0, 4) = (6, 4)$ (b) $f(1, 3) = (5, 3)$

    (c) $f(3, 2) = (3, 2)$ (d) $f(7, 1) = ({}^{-}1, 1)$

    (e) See Figure D. In each case the image and the object are equidistant from, and on opposite sides of, the line $x = 3$. Thus the function is self-inverse, and

$$f^{-1} : (x, y) \rightarrow (6 - x, y).$$

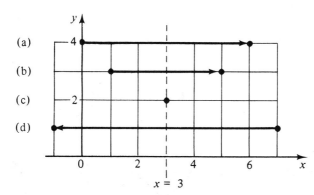

Figure D

5   (a) $\begin{bmatrix} {}^{-}2 \\ 5 \end{bmatrix}$ (b) $\begin{bmatrix} 3x + 2y \\ y \end{bmatrix}$

3.2 Reflection and symmetry

1   AB is the line of symmetry.

2   In (a), (d) and (e) the lines are lines of symmetry.

59

3 (a) See Figure E.

(b) Yes.

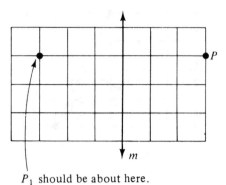

P_1 should be about here.

Figure E

4 (a) The image also moves towards the mirror.

(b) The image is also 60 cm from the mirror.

(c) The line is at right angles to the mirror, and is bisected by the mirror.

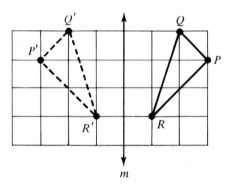

Figure F

 5 (a) See Figure F.

(b) The image of the triangle PQR is the triangle $P'Q'R'$.

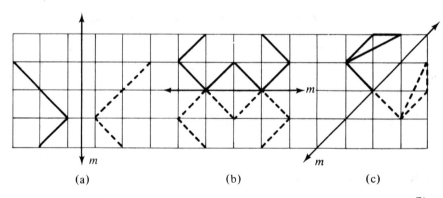

(a)   (b)   (c)

Figure G

6 See Figure G.

60

7 (a) The image of P' is P.

(b) The image of Q' is Q.

8 See Figure H.

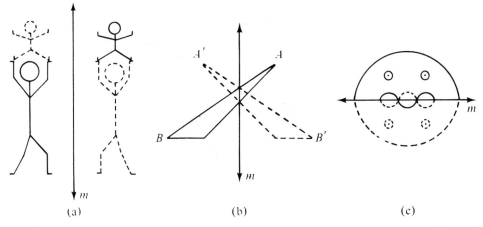

(a)   (b)   (c)

Figure H

Note from (b) that when an object line crosses the mirror it will intersect its image on the mirror. This is because the point on the mirror reflects into itself.

Exercise A

1 The lines in (a), (c) and (d) are lines of symmetry.

2 See Figure I.

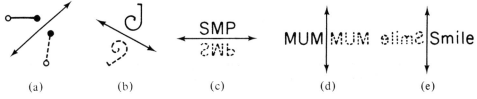

(a)   (b)   (c)   (d)   (e)

Figure I

3 Only one mirror line is possible, the perpendicular bisector of the line joining A to B.

4 (a) $35°$ (b) $90°$ (c) $55°$ (d) $110°$ (The original size of the angle BAB' was $70°$. When BAB' is a straight line the angle BAB' is $180°$.)

▶ **5** See Figure J.

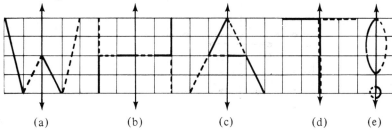

(a)   (b)   (c)   (d)   (e)   Figure J

6 (a) 24°

(b) The mirror line bisects the angle where the two lines (produced) meet. It is also the perpendicular bisector of both PP' and QQ' (see Figure K).

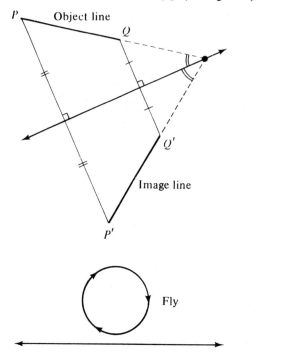

Figure K

Figure L

7 See Figure L. The fly's image travels round in an anti-clockwise direction. Both fly and image finish at the same time!

3.3 Reflections using coordinates

1 (a) See Figure M.

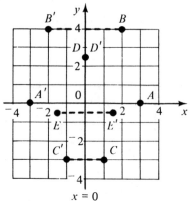

Figure M

(b) A' is $(^-3, 0)$, B' is $(^-2, 4)$, C' is $(^-1, ^-3)$, D' is $(0, 2\frac{1}{2})$ and E' is $(1\frac{1}{2}, ^-\frac{1}{2})$.

(c) The mirror is the mediator of each line segment.

(d) The image of Z will be $(^-x, y)$.

2 (a) See Figure N.

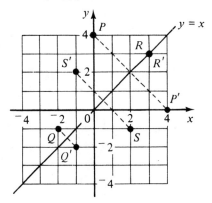

Figure N

(b) P is $(0, 4)$, Q is $(^-2, ^-1)$, R is $(3, 3)$, and S is $(2, ^-1)$.
   P' is $(4, 0)$, Q' is $(^-1, ^-2)$, R' is $(3, 3)$, and S' is $(^-1, 2)$.

(c) From (b) it should be apparent that the x and y coordinates are interchanged to give the image. Hence Z' is (y, x).

3 (a) and (b) See Figure O.

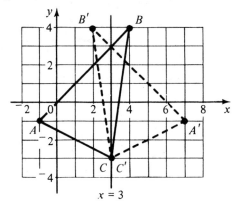

$x = 3$

Figure O

(c) AB and $A'B'$ meet on the mirror, at the point $(3, 3)$.

(d) See Figure P. Since $Z'N = ZN$, the x coordinate of Z' is $3 - k$. The y coordinate is unchanged.

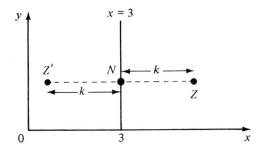

Figure P

63

Exercise B

1 (a) See Figure Q.   (b) Z' is (x, ⁻y).

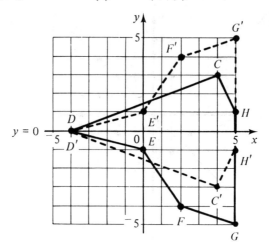

Figure Q

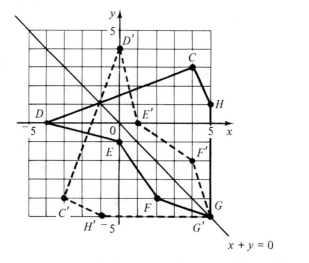

x + y = 0   Figure R

2 (a) See Figure R.   (b) Z' is (⁻y, ⁻x).

3.4 Matrix representation

1

$$\begin{matrix} A' & B' & C' & D' & E' \\ \begin{bmatrix} ^-3 & ^-2 & ^-1 & 0 & 1\frac{1}{2} \\ 0 & 4 & ^-3 & 2\frac{1}{2} & ^-\frac{1}{2} \end{bmatrix} \end{matrix}$$

2 (a) The image of Z is Z' (y, x).

(b) Hence $\begin{bmatrix} x' \\ y' \end{bmatrix} = \begin{bmatrix} y \\ x \end{bmatrix} = \begin{bmatrix} 0 & 1 \\ 1 & 0 \end{bmatrix} \begin{bmatrix} x \\ y \end{bmatrix}$ and so the matrix is $\begin{bmatrix} 0 & 1 \\ 1 & 0 \end{bmatrix}$.

64

(c)

$$\begin{array}{cccc} & P & Q & R & S \\ \begin{bmatrix} 0 & 1 \\ 1 & 0 \end{bmatrix} & \begin{bmatrix} 0 & ^-2 & 3 & 2 \\ 4 & ^-1 & 3 & ^-1 \end{bmatrix} \end{array} = \begin{array}{cccc} P' & Q' & R' & S' \\ \begin{bmatrix} 4 & ^-1 & 3 & ^-1 \\ 0 & ^-2 & 3 & 2 \end{bmatrix} \end{array}$$

3   In each case the answer is $\begin{bmatrix} 0 \\ 0 \end{bmatrix}$.

Exercise C

1   (a) For the mirror line $y = 0$, the image of (x, y) is $(x, {}^-y)$. Hence the matrix will be $\begin{bmatrix} 1 & 0 \\ 0 & ^-1 \end{bmatrix}$.

   (b) For the mirror line $x + y = 0$, the image is $({}^-y, {}^-x)$ and so the matrix is $\begin{bmatrix} 0 & ^-1 \\ ^-1 & 0 \end{bmatrix}$.

2   (a)

$$\begin{bmatrix} ^-0.6 & 0.8 \\ 0.8 & 0.6 \end{bmatrix} \begin{array}{ccc} P & Q & R \\ \begin{bmatrix} ^-2 & 2 & 5 \\ 1 & 4 & 0 \end{bmatrix} \end{array} = \begin{array}{ccc} P' & Q' & R' \\ \begin{bmatrix} 2 & 2 & ^-3 \\ ^-1 & 4 & 4 \end{bmatrix} \end{array}$$

   (b) See Figure S. This matrix represents reflection in the line OQ, i.e. the line $y = 2x$. Note that as Q is invariant (and O must be invariant as a 2×2 matrix is used) if the transformation is a reflection, then the mirror line is OQ. Remember also that the mirror line must pass through the intersection of a line and its image, and through the mid-point of the segment joining a point to its image.

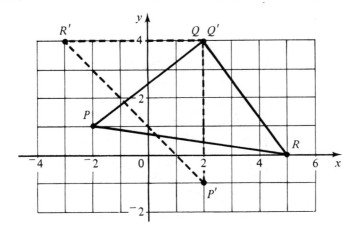

Figure S

3.5 Properties of reflection

1   All the properties listed, except position, are invariant under reflection.

2   In question 2 of Exercise C, the triangle PQR is lettered clockwise, but the image $P'Q'R'$ is anti-clockwise. Hence sense is not invariant under reflection. (Remember that, as in most 'rules', the result must be true in *all* cases for it to count.)

3   If you look at your answers to questions 1 and 2 of Exercise B, you will see that EF is parallel to CH in the object, and in both questions $E'F'$ is parallel to $C'H'$. This, and your other answers, should suggest that parallelism *is* invariant under reflection.

1 See Figure T.

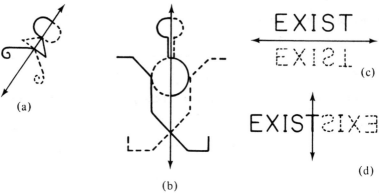

(a)

(b)

(c)

(d)

Figure T

2 (a) See Figure U.

(b)

$$\begin{bmatrix} 0 & 1 \\ 1 & 0 \end{bmatrix} \begin{array}{cccccc} O & A & B & C & D \\ \begin{bmatrix} 0 & 2 & 3 & 5 & 9 \\ 0 & 6 & 9 & 5 & 7 \end{bmatrix} \end{array} = \begin{array}{cccccc} O' & A' & B' & C' & D' \\ \begin{bmatrix} 0 & 6 & 9 & 5 & 7 \\ 0 & 2 & 3 & 5 & 9 \end{bmatrix} \end{array}$$

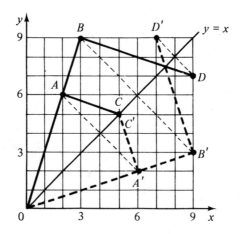

Figure U

3 (a) See Figure V.

(b)

$$\begin{array}{cc} & \begin{array}{ccccc} O & A & B & C & D \end{array} \end{array}$$

$$\begin{bmatrix} 0.6 & 0.8 \\ 0.8 & ^-0.6 \end{bmatrix} \begin{bmatrix} 0 & 2 & 3 & 5 & 9 \\ 0 & 6 & 9 & 5 & 7 \end{bmatrix} = \begin{bmatrix} 0 & 6 & 9 & 7 & 11 \\ 0 & ^-2 & ^-3 & 1 & 3 \end{bmatrix}$$

$$\begin{array}{ccccc} O' & A' & B' & C' & D' \end{array}$$

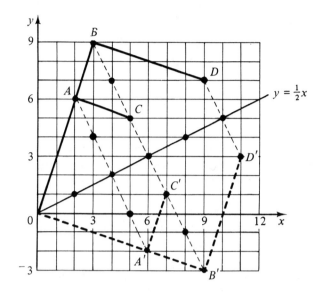

Figure V

4 (a) $x = 2$ (b) None (c) $y = x$ (d) $x = 5$

5 See Figure W. The stages in the solution are as follows. Draw and produce the line $P'Q$ to meet m at X, draw PQ to meet m at Y, then draw PX, and finally draw and produce $P'Y$ to meet PX at Q'.

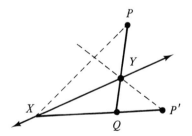

Figure W

As Q' is the image of Q, then Q is the image of Q' and so PQ' will be the image of $P'Q$. A line and its image meet on the mirror line, therefore PQ' meets $P'Q$ at X. Similarly PQ meets $P'Q'$ at Y, and so Q' is the intersection of PX and $P'Y$.

4 Rotation

Objectives

This is what you should be able to do after studying this chapter.
(1) Rotate a given figure about a point using tracing paper, protractor and compasses, or – in certain cases – coordinates and/or matrices.
(2) Know that this particular transformation is a direct isometry, i.e. that size, shape and sense are unaltered under rotation.
(3) Know that if a figure has been rotated through $\theta°$ then the angle between any line (in the original figure) and its image is also $\theta°$.
(4) Find the centre and angle of rotation, given an object and its image.
(5) State the coordinates of the images of the point (x, y) under rotations of 90°, 180° and 270°, and the matrices for these rotations when the centre of rotation is at the origin.
(6) State the inverse of a given rotation.

Pre-test

▷ 1 Measure the angles marked in Figure 1, parts (a), (b) and (c).

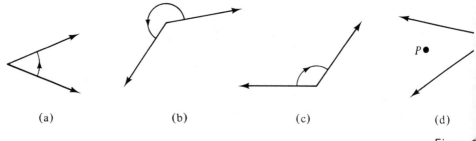

(a)　　　　　　　　(b)　　　　　　　　(c)　　　　　　　　(d)

Figure 1

2 Trace Figure 1(d).
  (a) Produce each line until they cross, and measure the acute angle between the lines.
  (b) Draw the perpendiculars from P to the two lines, and measure the acute angle between these. What do you find?

3 A triangular flag F has coordinates (2, 1), (2, 3), (2, 4) and (4, 3).
  (a) Draw the flag F on graph paper (draw axes for values of x from $^-5$ to 5, and values of y from 0 to 5).
  (b) Draw F_1, the image of F after reflection in the y axis (the line $x = 0$).
  (c) State a mapping for $F \rightarrow F_1$ in the form $(x, y) \rightarrow (\ , \ )$.
  (d) Write down the matrix that represents this transformation.

4.1 Some investigations

> 1 Place two coins of the same size on a table. Keep one coin, A, fixed. Rotate the other coin, B, around it without slipping, starting in the position shown in Figure 2(a) with its head upright. When it gets to the position of Figure 2(b), is its head upright or upside down? Through what angle has B turned by the time it returns to its original position?

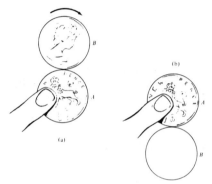

Figure 2

2 As you ride a bicycle along a flat road, what is the locus (the path traced out by a point) of
  (a) the head of a drawing pin sticking in the tyre,
  (b) the valve of one of the tyres?

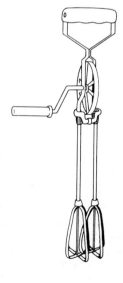

3 Take a look at a kitchen beater (see Figure 3). Do the two rotating parts rotate in the same direction? Why don't they get tangled up?

Figure 3

4 Cut out any shape from a piece of card and place it on a sheet of plain paper. Put a pin through it at some point O and make a small hole for a pencil to go through at another point P (see Figure 4). Rotate the cut-out and mark the path of P with the pencil.

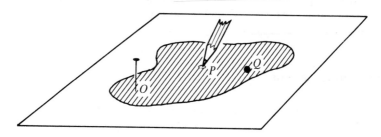

Figure 4

(a) What is the locus of P?
(b) If Q is any other point on the cut-out what can you say about the locus of Q as the cut-out is rotated?

3

All these four examples involve *rotation* in some form. Rotation – the turning of an object about some point (the *centre of rotation*) into a new (image) position – is another transformation.

Examples **1** and **2** above are complicated by the fact that the centres of rotation (the centre of the coin B, and the centre of the bicycle wheel) are themselves moving. In this book we shall consider only rotations whose centre is a fixed point.

4.2 Rotation about a given centre

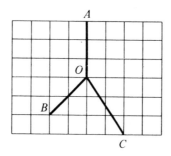

Figure 5

1 Trace the shape in Figure 5. Leave the tracing paper in position and, with a pin or a compass point, rotate the tracing paper about O so that OA is turned through an angle of 90°.
(a) Through what angle has OB been rotated?
(b) Through what angle has OC been rotated?
(c) If OA had been rotated through 60°, through what angle would OB and OC have turned?

4

2   Using tracing paper again, roate the T in Figure 6 about the point O.

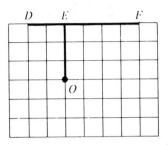

Figure 6

What is the angle between the old and the new directions of DEF, if OE is rotated through (a) $90°$, (b) $30°$?

When you rotated your tracing paper through $60°$ (or $30°$ or $90°$) did you rotate it clockwise or anti-clockwise? It is obviously desirable that people should agree as to which way is to be regarded as positive. The convention is that an anti-clockwise rotation is positive, and a clockwise rotation is negative. (A convention is a man-made rule – an agreement so that all (or most) people do the same thing, such as driving on the left-hand side of the road in Britain.)

3   (a) For what angle of rotation does the direction not matter?
     (b) What positive rotation will have the same effect as a rotation of $^-100°$?

4   Copy Figure 7. Trace the figure and rotate the tracing paper about C until G lies on the line CD. Dot through the new positions of G, H and F, label them G_1, H_1 and F_1, and join up the triangle $F_1G_1H_1$.

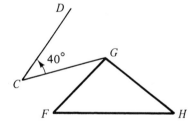

Figure 7

You have now rotated the triangle FGH through $40°$ about the point C. $F_1G_1H_1$ is the image of FGH under this rotation.

Exercise A

1   Copy Figure 8 (overleaf), and on your diagram draw the images of
    (a) AB when rotated through $^+90°$ about O_1,
    (b) CD when rotated through $^+90°$ about O_2,
    (c) EF when rotated through $^-90°$ about O_3.

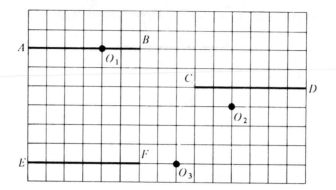

Figure 8

2   Copy Figure 9 and use compasses and protractor to construct the image of the triangle *FGH* when rotated through 60° about *O*. (Hint. Join *OF* and draw a line through *O* at 60° to this line, put the compass point on *O* and draw an arc from *F* to meet this line at F_1, etc.)

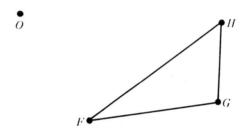

Figure 9

What is the angle between the old and new positions of (a) *FG*, (b) *GH*, (c) *HF*?

3   State another angle of rotation that would have the same effect as a rotation of
(a) 35°, (b) 315°, (c) ⁻42°, (d) ⁻148°.

4   (a) On squared paper draw *x* and *y* axes from ⁻4 to 4 and mark the origin *O* and the points $A(2, 1)$, $B(3, 4)$, $C(^-2, 3)$, $D(^-3, ^-1)$, $E(2, ^-2)$ and $F(0, 1)$.
    (b) Using tracing paper, rotate these six points through 180° about *O*. What are the coordinates of the images?
    (c) What happens to the coordinates each time? Write down the coordinates of the image of the point (x, y).

5   Using the same diagram as for question **4**, repeat that question for a rotation of 90°.

6   If the shaded square in Figure 10 is rotated through 180° about *O* it will map onto the unshaded square.

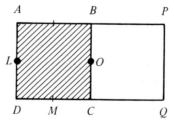

Figure 10

(a) Copy the diagram and draw the loci of C, D and M under this rotation.

(b) What other centres of rotation could be used to map one square onto the other? Give the angle of rotation, and the images of A, B, C and D in each case.

(c) Describe two other single transformations that map the shaded square onto the unshaded square.

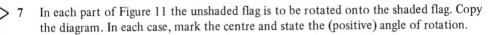

> 7 In each part of Figure 11 the unshaded flag is to be rotated onto the shaded flag. Copy the diagram. In each case, mark the centre and state the (positive) angle of rotation.

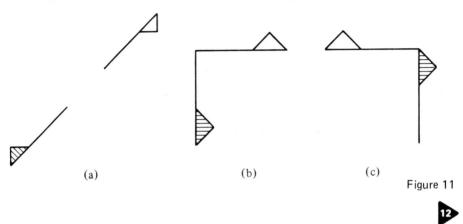

(a)   (b)   (c)

Figure 11

4.3 The centre of a rotation

In the last question of the previous exercise it was fairly easy to find the centre of rotation by 'trial and error'.

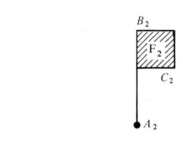

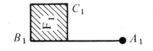

Figure 12

> 1 Trace the left-hand flag (F_1) in Figure 12 and try to find, by trial and error, the centre of the rotation that maps F_1 onto F_2.

2 Add the flag F_2 to your tracing. Fold and crease your tracing paper so that A_1 folds over onto A_2. Repeat for the points B_1 and B_2, and for C_1 and C_2. What do you find?

73

Figure 13 is a copy of Figure 12, but showing now the centre of rotation O, the constru
tion lines for finding the images of A_1 and C_1, and the creases that you should have
obtained on your tracing paper.

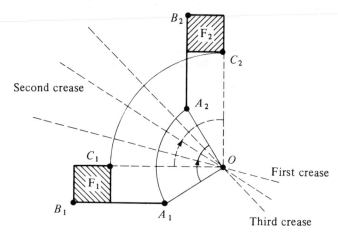

Angles A_1OA_2, B_1OB_2, C_1OC_2, ... are all $90°$ – the angle of the rotation

Figure 13

If A_1 is to be mapped onto A_2 by a rotation about some point X, then A_1X is equal to
A_2X in length, and an alternative transformation to map A_1 (or A_1X) onto A_2 (or A_2X) is
a reflection whose mirror line is the bisector of angle A_1XA_2. (See Figure 14.)

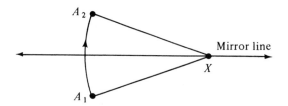

Figure 14

The creases on your tracing paper are really mirror lines for reflecting one point onto
another. Thus the centre of *any* rotation that maps A_1 onto A_2 must lie somewhere on
the mirror line of *the* reflection that maps A_1 onto A_2 (i.e. on the mediator of A_1A_2).
Thus *any* point on the first crease on your tracing paper can be used as a centre to rotate
A_1 onto A_2, as can *any* point on the second crease to rotate B_1 onto B_2, and so on. But
if we want to rotate A_1, B_1, C_1, ... onto A_2, B_2, C_2, ... *simultaneously*, the centre must
lie on all of these creases, and so must be the point at which they all meet.

Thus to find the centre of rotation in a diagram such as Figure 12 we construct the
mediators of A_1A_2, B_1B_2, C_1C_2, ... and the point where they meet is the centre of
rotation. In theory, two such mediators are sufficient to find the centre of rotation. In
practice, it is better to use three – if possible making angles of about $45°-60°$ with each
other.

Exercise B

1 Copy Figure 15 and find the centres for these rotations.
   (a) $S_1 \rightarrow S_2$ (b) $S_1 \rightarrow S_3$ (c) $S_2 \rightarrow S_3$ (d) $S_3 \rightarrow S_1$

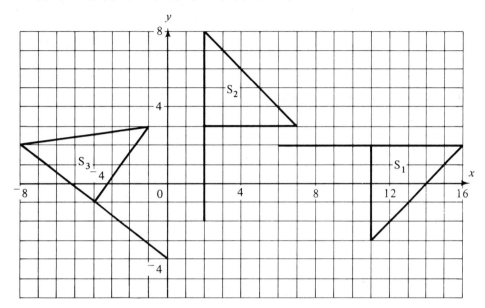

Figure 15

2 For which parts of Figure 16 is it possible to map one F onto the other F by a rotation?

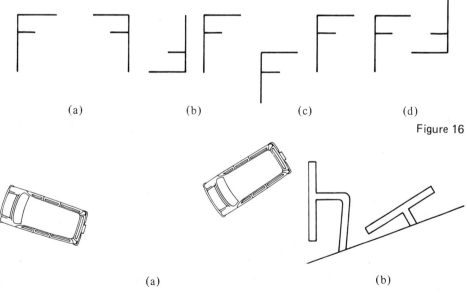

(a)   (b)   (c)   (d)

Figure 16

(a)   (b)

Figure 17

3   (a) Figure 17(a) shows a bird's eye view of two different positions of a lorry as it is being driven round a roundabout. Find the centre of the roundabout, and its approximate radius given that the lorry is 8 metres long.

    (b) Figure 17(b) shows the visible part of the brake pedal in a car in two positions. About which point is the brake pedal pivoted?

4.4 Matrix representation

The image of (x, y) under rotations about the origin

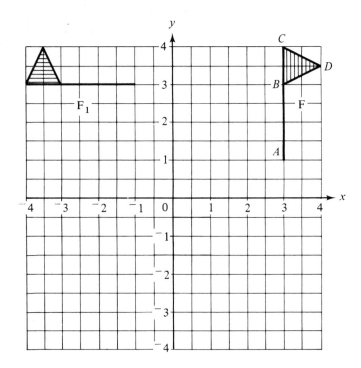

Figure 18

Figure 18 shows a flag F, and its image F_1 under a rotation of 90° (anti-clockwise) about the origin.

1   (a) Use tracing paper to confirm that F_1 is the image under this transformation.

    (b) Write down the coordinates of the images of A, B, C and D under this transformation.

    (c) State what has happened to the x and y coordinates of each point of the object.

    (d) Copy and complete the following statement.

$$(x, y) \xrightarrow[\text{about the origin}]{\text{under a rotation of 90°}} (\quad , \quad),$$

i.e. $\begin{bmatrix} x \\ y \end{bmatrix} \longrightarrow \begin{bmatrix} \quad \end{bmatrix}.$

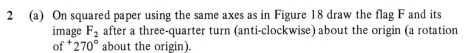

2 (a) On squared paper using the same axes as in Figure 18 draw the flag F and its image F_2 after a three-quarter turn (anti-clockwise) about the origin (a rotation of $^+270°$ about the origin).

(b) Write down the coordinates of the images of A, B, C and D.

(c) Express the mapping in the form

$$\begin{bmatrix} x \\ y \end{bmatrix} \rightarrow \begin{bmatrix} \ \\ \ \end{bmatrix}.$$

Finding the matrix

As in Chapter 3, we are looking for a 2 × 2 matrix $\mathbf{R}$ such that

$$\mathbf{R} \cdot \begin{bmatrix} x \\ y \end{bmatrix} = \begin{bmatrix} x' \\ y' \end{bmatrix},$$

where (x', y') is the image of the point (x, y) under a particular rotation.

Thus, for a (positive) quarter turn about the origin, since

$$\begin{bmatrix} x \\ y \end{bmatrix} \rightarrow \begin{bmatrix} ^-y \\ x \end{bmatrix}$$ (as shown in **1** above), we need a 2 × 2 matrix such that

$$\begin{bmatrix} \cdot & \cdot \\ \cdot & \cdot \end{bmatrix} \begin{bmatrix} x \\ y \end{bmatrix} = \begin{bmatrix} ^-y \\ x \end{bmatrix},$$

and it is not difficult to see that this is satisfied by

$$\begin{bmatrix} 0 & ^-1 \\ 1 & 0 \end{bmatrix} \begin{bmatrix} x \\ y \end{bmatrix} = \begin{bmatrix} ^-y \\ x \end{bmatrix}.$$

Hence the matrix that represents a quarter turn about the origin is

$$\begin{bmatrix} 0 & ^-1 \\ 1 & 0 \end{bmatrix}.$$

3 Use the results of **2** above to find the matrix for a (positive) three-quarter turn about the origin.

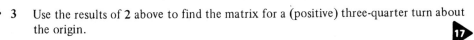

The inverse of a given rotation

4 Look back at Figure 18.

(a) What transformation maps F_1 onto F? What is the inverse of a rotation through $^+90°$ about the origin?

(b) What is the matrix for this inverse transformation?

(c) Is this matrix the inverse of the matrix for the original transformation?

5 What is the inverse of a three-quarter turn about some point Q?

Exercise C

1 What is the matrix for a rotation of 360° about the origin?

2   State the inverses of the following.
   (a) A rotation of $100°$ about the point $(5, 0)$.
   (b) A rotation of $200°$ about the point $(3, 7)$.
   (c) A rotation of $120°$ clockwise about the point $(1, 1)$.

3   (a) Repeat question 2 of Section 4.4 for a half turn – a rotation of $180°$ about the
      origin.
   (b) Hence find the matrix for this transformation.
   (c) What is special about this particular rotation?

Summary

(1) Figure 19 shows what happens when the shape *ABCDEF* is rotated about the centre *O*,
through an angle of $\theta°$.

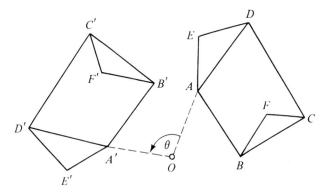

Figure 19

(2) (a) *O* is called the centre of rotation.
    (b) θ is called the angle of rotation. It is measured anti-clockwise.

(3) The figure and its image are directly congruent under rotation. Thus they have the
same shape, the same size, and the same sense.

(4) Every line is turned through the same angle ($\theta°$) by the rotation. Thus, if an object
and its image under a rotation are given, the angle of rotation is the angle between any
line and its image (produced if necessary).

(5) The centre of rotation *O* is equidistant from *A* and *A′*, *B* and *B′*, *C* and *C′*, etc. Hence if
an object and its image under a rotation are given, the centre of rotation will be at the
intersection of the mediators of *AA′*, *BB′*, *CC′*, etc.

(6) The images of the point (x, y) under certain rotations about the origin, and the
matrices for these rotations are as follows.

Angle of rotation	$^+90°$	$^+180°$	$^+270°$
Image of (x, y)	$(^-y, x)$	$(^-x, ^-y)$	$(y, ^-x)$
Matrix	$\begin{bmatrix} 0 & ^-1 \\ 1 & 0 \end{bmatrix}$	$\begin{bmatrix} ^-1 & 0 \\ 0 & ^-1 \end{bmatrix}$	$\begin{bmatrix} 0 & 1 \\ ^-1 & 0 \end{bmatrix}$

(7) A rotation of $0°$ or $360°$ (or $720°$ etc.) is an identity rotation, as the object is mapped back onto itself. Hence the inverse of a rotation of $\theta°$ about a centre C is a rotation of $^-\theta°$ about the same centre C.

Post-test

> 1 P is the quadrilateral $A(1, 2), B(2\frac{1}{2}, 1), C(3, 2)$ and $D(3, 4)$. $\mathbf{R_1}$ (P) is the image of P under a rotation of $180°$ about the origin, $\mathbf{R_2}$ (P) is the image of P under a rotation of $90°$ (anti-clockwise) about the point $(1\frac{1}{2}, ^-\frac{1}{2})$, and $\mathbf{R_3}$ (P) is the image of P under a rotation of $^-90°$ about the point $(0, 1)$.
Draw x and y axes for values of x and y from $^-4$ to 4, and on these axes draw P, $\mathbf{R_1}$ (P), $\mathbf{R_2}$ (P) and $\mathbf{R_3}$ (P).

2 From your diagram for question 1 find the centre and angle of the rotation that maps (a) $\mathbf{R_2}$(P) onto $\mathbf{R_3}$(P),   (b) $\mathbf{R_3}$(P) onto $\mathbf{R_1}$ (P).

3 A letter L is formed by the points $(^-1, \frac{1}{2}), (^-1, ^-1), (1, ^-1), (1, ^-\frac{1}{2}), (^-\frac{1}{2}, ^-\frac{1}{2})$ and $(^-\frac{1}{2}, \frac{1}{2})$. Under a certain rotation the images of the first two points are $(1\frac{1}{2}, 1)$ and $(3, 1)$ respectively.
(a) Plot these points on a diagram (take values of x and y from $^-2$ to 4).
(b) Find the centre and the angle of this rotation.
(c) Draw the complete image on your diagram.

4 Figure 20 shows a shape E and its image $\mathbf{R}(E)$ under a rotation. Trace the diagram. By constructing the mediators of AA_1, BB_1 and CC_1 find the centre of rotation O. Measure the angles AOA_1, BOB_1 and COC_1. What is the angle of the rotation?

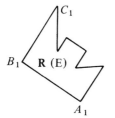
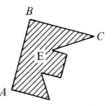

Figure 20

5 (a) With x and y axes from 0 to 10 plot the triangle Z whose vertices are $A(5, 0)$, $B(10, 0)$ and $C(10, 5)$.
(b) Find the images of A, B and C under the transformation whose matrix is
$$M = \begin{bmatrix} 0.8 & ^-0.6 \\ 0.6 & 0.8 \end{bmatrix}.$$
(c) Plot $\mathbf{M}(Z)$ on your diagram.
(d) Does M represent a rotation? If so, state its centre, and find the angle of the rotation.

Assignment

1 Trace Figure 21. Find the following by construction.
(a) The image of the shape S when rotated through $^-120°$ about the point P.
(b) The centre and angle of the rotation that maps S onto T.

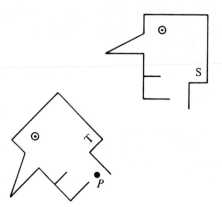

Figure 21

2   Draw x and y axes for values of x and y from $^-1$ to 5.
    (a) On these axes plot the triangle T whose vertices are $(2, {}^-1), (2, 2)$ and $(3, {}^-1)$
        and its image under a rotation of $180°$ about the point $(1, 1)$.
    (b) Draw the triangle V whose vertices are $(1, 3), (4, 3)$ and $(4, 4)$. Find the centre,
        and angle of rotation, of the rotation that maps T onto V.

3   Write down the matrices representing rotations of a quarter turn, half turn, and three-
    quarter turn about the origin. If the vertices of a square are $(1, 1), (1, 2), (2, 2)$ and
    $(2, 1)$ use multiplication by the appropriate matrix to find the vertices of the images
    of this square under each rotation. Show the original square and its three images on a
    diagram.

Answers

Pre-test

 1   (a) $43°$ (b) $180° + 45° = 225°$ (or $360° - 135° = 225°$)   (c) $126°$

2   (a) $47°$ (b) $47°$. Both angles are the same (see Figure A).

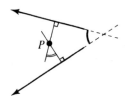

Figure A

3   (a) and (b) See Figure B.
    (c) $F \rightarrow F_1$ is $(x, y) \rightarrow ({}^-x, y)$.
    (d) $\begin{bmatrix} {}^-1 & 0 \\ 0 & 1 \end{bmatrix}$

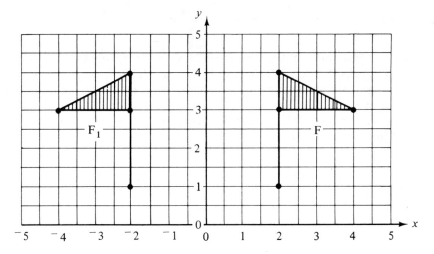

Figure B

4.1 Some investigations

2 ▶ **1**   Upright. After going around the fixed coin once, B has turned through two turns of $360°$.

2   See Figure C. The height d is the diameter of the wheel, and the length c is the circumference of the wheel.

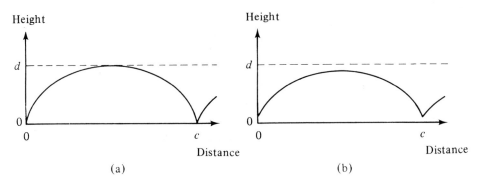

Figure C

3   The two rotating parts rotate in opposite directions. They rotate at the same speed, and are $45°$ 'out of phase'.

3 ▶ **4**   The *loci* (plural of *locus*) of P and Q are circles with centres at O.

4.2 Rotation about a given centre

▶ **1**   (a) and (b) OB and OC are also rotated through $90°$.
   (c) OB and OC would also have turned through $60°$.

(a) The angle between *DEF* and its image is also 90°.

(b) The angle is 30°.

6

3 (a) 180°, a half turn. In this case it doesn't matter whether you turn clockwise or anti-clockwise if it is only the final position which is of interest. However, a regimental sergeant-major would not be too pleased if some of his men turned clockwise and some anti-clockwise on the command 'About...turn!', and so a convention (of 'right about turn' – clockwise) is necessary again here.

(b) $^+260°$. See Figure D.

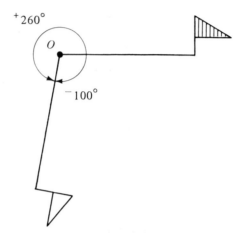

Figure D

7

4 See Figure E.

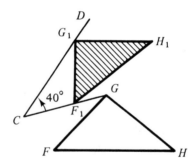

Figure E

Exercise A

1 See Figure F.

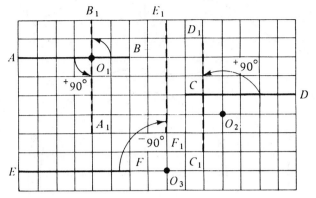

Figure F

2 See Figure G. In each case the angle between a side of the triangle and its image is 60°.

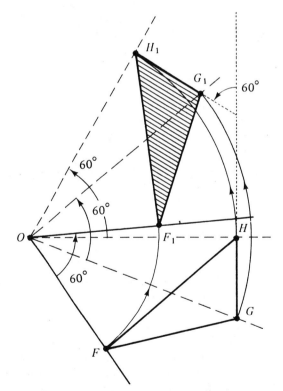

Figure G

3 (a) $^-325°$ (or $395°$, $755°$, and so on – any angle that is $35° \pm$ a multiple of $360°$)
(b) $45°$ (c) $318°$ (d) $212°$

4 (a) See Figure H.

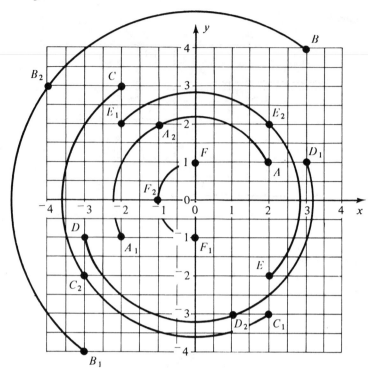

Figure H

(b) See Figure H.

$A(2, 1) \rightarrow A_1(^-2, ^-1)$ $D(^-3, ^-1) \rightarrow D_1(3, 1)$
$B(3, 4) \rightarrow B_1(^-3, ^-4)$ $E(2, ^-2) \rightarrow E_1(^-2, 2)$
$C(^-2, 3) \rightarrow C_1(2, ^-3)$ $F(0, 1) \rightarrow F_1(0, ^-1)$

(c) In each case the signs of both the x and the y coordinates are changed. Hence the image of the point (x, y) is the point $(^-x, ^-y)$.

5 See Figure H.

$A(2, 1) \rightarrow A_2(^-1, 2)$ $D(^-3, ^-1) \rightarrow D_2(1, ^-3)$
$B(3, 4) \rightarrow B_2(^-4, 3)$ $E(2, ^-2) \rightarrow E_2(2, 2)$
$C(^-2, 3) \rightarrow C_2(^-3, ^-2)$ $F(0, 1) \rightarrow F_2(^-1, 0)$.

The x coordinate of the image is negative the y coordinate of the object, and the y coordinate of the image is the x coordinate of the object. Hence the image of (x, y) is the point $(^-y, x)$.

6 (a) See Figure I. C, D and M rotate onto B, P and M_1 respectively.
  (b) With B as centre, a quarter turn will rotate A, B, C, D onto C, B, P, Q, respectively. With C as centre, a three-quarter turn (or a negative quarter turn) will map A, B, C, D onto P, Q, C, B respectively.
  (c) A translation will map A, B, C, D onto B, P, Q, C respectively. A reflection in the line BC will map A, B, C, D onto P, B, C, Q respectively.

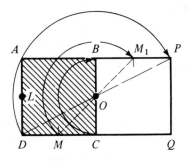

Figure I

There are also three combinations of a reflection followed by a translation that will give a different orientation of the image. Such *combined transformations* are considered in *Further Matrices and Transformations*. This gives a total of eight ways in which the shaded square can be mapped onto the other square. If the shaded square were cut out of the page, there are eight ways in which it could be placed on the unshaded square.

7 See Figure J.

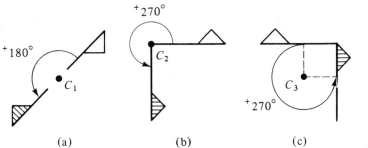

(a)   (b)   (c)   Figure J

4.3 The centre of a rotation

1 and 2 are answered in the text. See Figure 13.

Exercise B

1 (a) $(6, ^-2)$ (b) $(4, ^-2)$ (c) $(3, ^-5)$ (d) $(4, ^-2)$ (same as (b)).
The construction for (b) is shown in Figure K overleaf.

2 The transformation is a rotation in parts (b) and (d). (In (a) it is a reflection and in (c) it is a translation.) See Figure L overleaf.

3 See Figure M overleaf. In part (a) it is not easy to be very accurate as the 'angle of rotation' from one position of the lorry to the other is small. The two mediators shown in Figure M(a) are chosen so as to make the angle between them as large as possible.

As OA is approximately $2\frac{1}{3}$ times the length of AB, the radius of the inside of the roundabout will be about 19 metres.

85

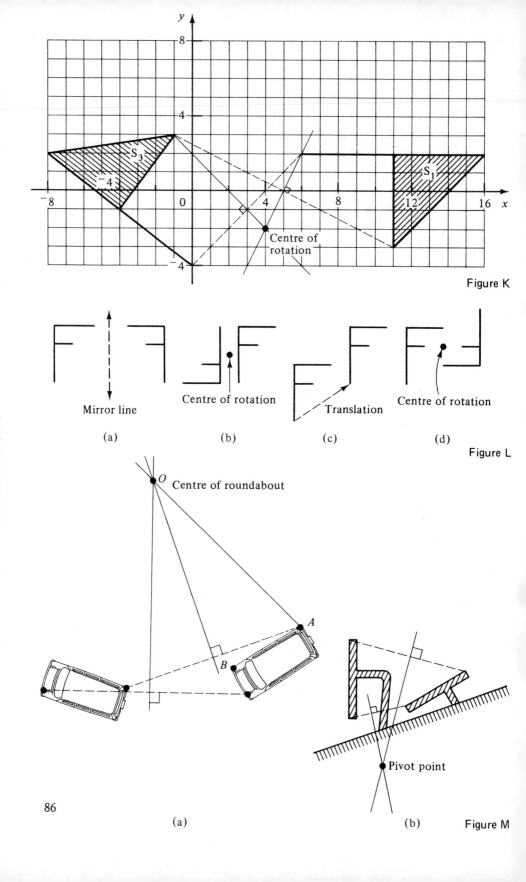

Figure K

Mirror line

Centre of rotation

Translation

Centre of rotation

(a)

(b)

(c)

(d)

Figure L

O Centre of roundabout

A

B

Pivot point

86

(a)

(b)

Figure M

4.4 Matrix representation

5 **1** (b) $A(3, 1) \rightarrow A_1(^-1, 3)$ $\qquad$ $B(3, 3) \rightarrow B_1(^-3, 3)$
$\qquad$ $C(3, 4) \rightarrow C_1(^-4, 3)$ $\qquad\qquad$ $D(4, 3\frac{1}{2}) \rightarrow D_1(^-3\frac{1}{2}, 4)$

(c) The x coordinate of each point of the object has become the y coordinate of the corresponding point of the image. The x coordinate of the image point is minus the y coordinate of the object point.

(d) Hence $(x, y) \rightarrow (^-y, x)$, i.e. $\begin{bmatrix} x \\ y \end{bmatrix} \rightarrow \begin{bmatrix} ^-y \\ x \end{bmatrix}$.

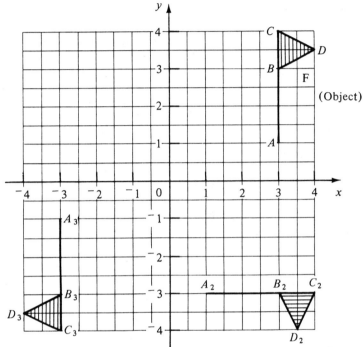

F_3. Image under $\frac{1}{2}$ turn $\qquad\qquad\qquad\qquad$ F_2: Image under $\frac{3}{4}$ turn

Figure N

6 **2** (a) See Figure N.

(b) $A \rightarrow (1, ^-3), B \rightarrow (3, ^-3), C \rightarrow (4, ^-3), D \rightarrow (3\frac{1}{2}, ^-4)$

(c) $\begin{bmatrix} x \\ y \end{bmatrix} \rightarrow \begin{bmatrix} y \\ ^-x \end{bmatrix}$

7 **3** From 2(c) above, in order to obtain the y, the top row of the matrix will be $\begin{bmatrix} 0 & 1 \end{bmatrix}$

$$\begin{bmatrix} 0 & 1 \\ \cdot & \cdot \end{bmatrix} \begin{bmatrix} x \\ y \end{bmatrix} = \begin{bmatrix} y \\ \cdot \end{bmatrix},$$

and to obtain the ^-x, the bottom row will be $\begin{bmatrix} ^-1 & 0 \end{bmatrix}$

$$\begin{bmatrix} \cdot & \cdot \\ ^-1 & 0 \end{bmatrix} \begin{bmatrix} x \\ y \end{bmatrix} = \begin{bmatrix} \cdot \\ ^-x \end{bmatrix},$$

and so the complete matrix is $\begin{bmatrix} 0 & 1 \\ ^-1 & 0 \end{bmatrix}$.

18

4 (a) A rotation of $^-90°$ (or $^+270°$) about the origin maps F_1 onto F. Thus this is the inverse of a rotation of $^+90°$ about the origin.

(b) The matrix is $\begin{bmatrix} 0 & 1 \\ ^-1 & 0 \end{bmatrix}$ from 3 above.

(c) This is the inverse of the matrix $\begin{bmatrix} 0 & ^-1 \\ 1 & 0 \end{bmatrix}$ for the original transformation.

5 The inverse of a three-quarter turn rotation is hence a negative three-quarter turn (or a positive quarter turn) about the same point Q.

Exercise C

19

1 A 360° rotation returns the object to its original position, and so is the identity. Hence its matrix is $\begin{bmatrix} 1 & 0 \\ 0 & 1 \end{bmatrix}$.

2 (a) A rotation of $^-100°$ (or $^+260°$) about the point (5, 0).
(b) A rotation of $^-200°$ (or $^+160°$) about the point (3, 7).
(c) A rotation of $^+120°$ (or $^-240°$) about the point (1, 1).

3 (a) See Figure N.
(b) In Exercise A, question 4, it was shown that the image of (x, y) under a half turn about the origin is $(^-x, ^-y)$. Hence the matrix is $\begin{bmatrix} ^-1 & 0 \\ 0 & ^-1 \end{bmatrix}$.
(c) The inverse of a half turn is another half turn, i.e. this particular rotation is self-inverse. (A half turn about any centre will also be self-inverse).

Post-test

20

1 See Figure O.

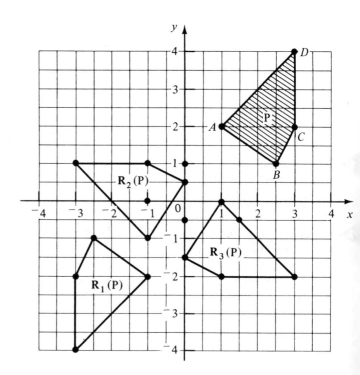

Figure O

88

2 (a) $\mathbf{R}_2(P) \rightarrow \mathbf{R}_3(P)$ is a half turn about the point $(0, -\tfrac{1}{2})$.

(b) $\mathbf{R}_3(P) \rightarrow \mathbf{R}_1(P)$ is a positive three-quarter turn (or a negative quarter turn) about the point $(^-1, 0)$.

3 See Figure P.

(b) The centre of the rotation is $(0, 2)$. It is a quarter turn.

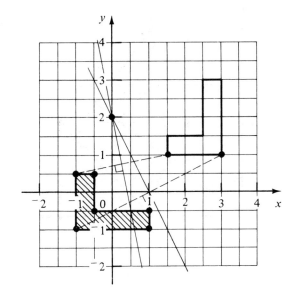

Figure P

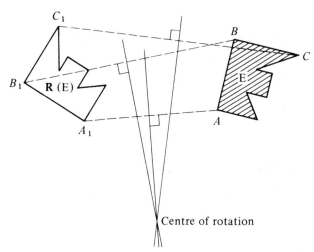

Centre of rotation

Figure Q

4 See Figure Q. The angle of rotation is between $65°$ and $70°$.

5 See Figure R.

(b)
$$\begin{array}{cc} & \\ \begin{bmatrix} 0.8 & {}^-0.6 \\ 0.6 & 0.8 \end{bmatrix} \end{array} \begin{array}{ccc} A & B & C \\ \begin{bmatrix} 5 & 10 & 10 \\ 0 & 0 & 5 \end{bmatrix} \end{array} = \begin{array}{ccc} A' & B' & C' \\ \begin{bmatrix} 4 & 8 & 5 \\ 3 & 6 & 10 \end{bmatrix} \end{array}.$$

(d) **M** is a rotation about the origin through an angle of approximately $37°$.

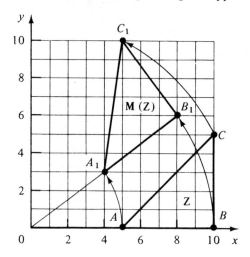

Figure R

Published by the Press Syndicate of the University of Cambridge
The Pitt Building, Trumpington Street, Cambridge CB2 1RP
32 East 57th Street, New York, NY 10022, USA
296 Beaconsfield Parade, Middle Park, Melbourne 3206, Australia

First published 1981

Typeset and illustrated by Reproduction Drawings Ltd, Sutton, Surrey
Printed in Great Britain at the University Press, Cambridge

British Library cataloguing in publication data

School Mathematics Project
Individualised mathematics.
Matrix algebra and isometric transformations
1. Mathematics – 1961 –
I. Title   II. National Extension College
510   QA39.2
ISBN 0 521 28265 9